THE LEGEND OF KORRA

Created by
BRYAN KONIETZKO
MICHAEL DANTE DiMARTINO

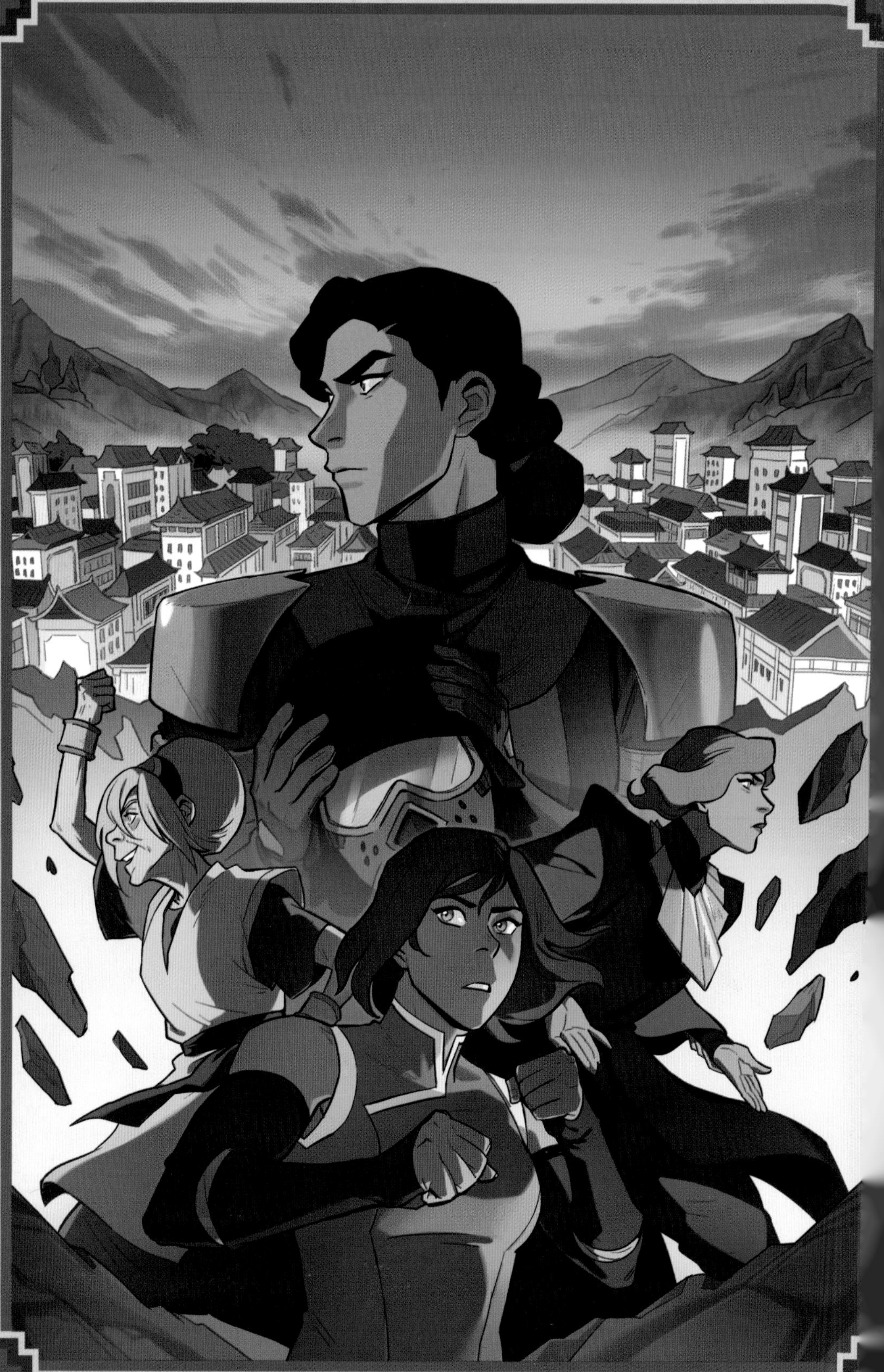

THE LEGEND OF KORRA

RUINS OF THE EMPIRE · PART TWO

written by
MICHAEL DANTE DiMARTINO

art by
MICHELLE WONG

colors by
KILLIAN NG

lettering by
RACHEL DEERING

cover by
MICHELLE WONG with **KILLIAN NG**

DARK HORSE BOOKS

president and publisher **MIKE RICHARDSON**

editor **RACHEL ROBERTS**   assistant editor **JENNY BLENK**   designer **SARAH TERRY**

digital art technicians **CHRISTIANNE GILLENARDO-GOUDREAU** and **SAMANTHA HUMMER**

Special thanks to Linda Lee, James Salerno, and Joan Hilty
at Nickelodeon, to Dave Marshall at Dark Horse, and to Bryan
Konietzko, Michael Dante DiMartino, and Tim Hedrick.

Published by **DARK HORSE BOOKS**
A division of Dark Horse Comics LLC
10956 SE Main Street, Milwaukie, OR 97222

DARKHORSE.COM | **NICK.COM**

Comic Shop Locator Service: comicshoplocator.com

First edition: October 2019 | ISBN 978-1-50670-895-9

1 3 5 7 9 10 8 6 4 2
Printed in China

Library of Congress Cataloging-in-Publication Data

Names: DiMartino, Michael Dante, writer, creator. | Wong, Michelle (Comic
  book artist), artist. | Ng, Killian, colourist, artist. | Deering, Rachel,
  1983- letterer.
Title: The legend of Korra : ruins of the empire / written by Michael Dante
  DiMartino ; art by Michelle Wong ; colors by Killian Ng ; lettering by
  Rachel Deering ; cover by Michelle Wong with Killian Ng.
Other titles: Legend of Korra (Television program)
Description: Milwaukie, OR : Dark Horse Books, 2019- | "Created by Bryan
  Konietzko, Michael Dante DiMartino"
Identifiers: LCCN 2018052018| ISBN 9781506708942 (part one : paperback) |
  ISBN 9781506708959 (part two : paperback)
Subjects: LCSH: Comic books, strips, etc. | BISAC: COMICS & GRAPHIC NOVELS /
  Media Tie-In. | COMICS & GRAPHIC NOVELS / Gay & Lesbian.
Classification: LCC PN6728.L434 D54 2019 | DDC 741.5/973--dc23
LC record available at https://lccn.loc.gov/2018052018

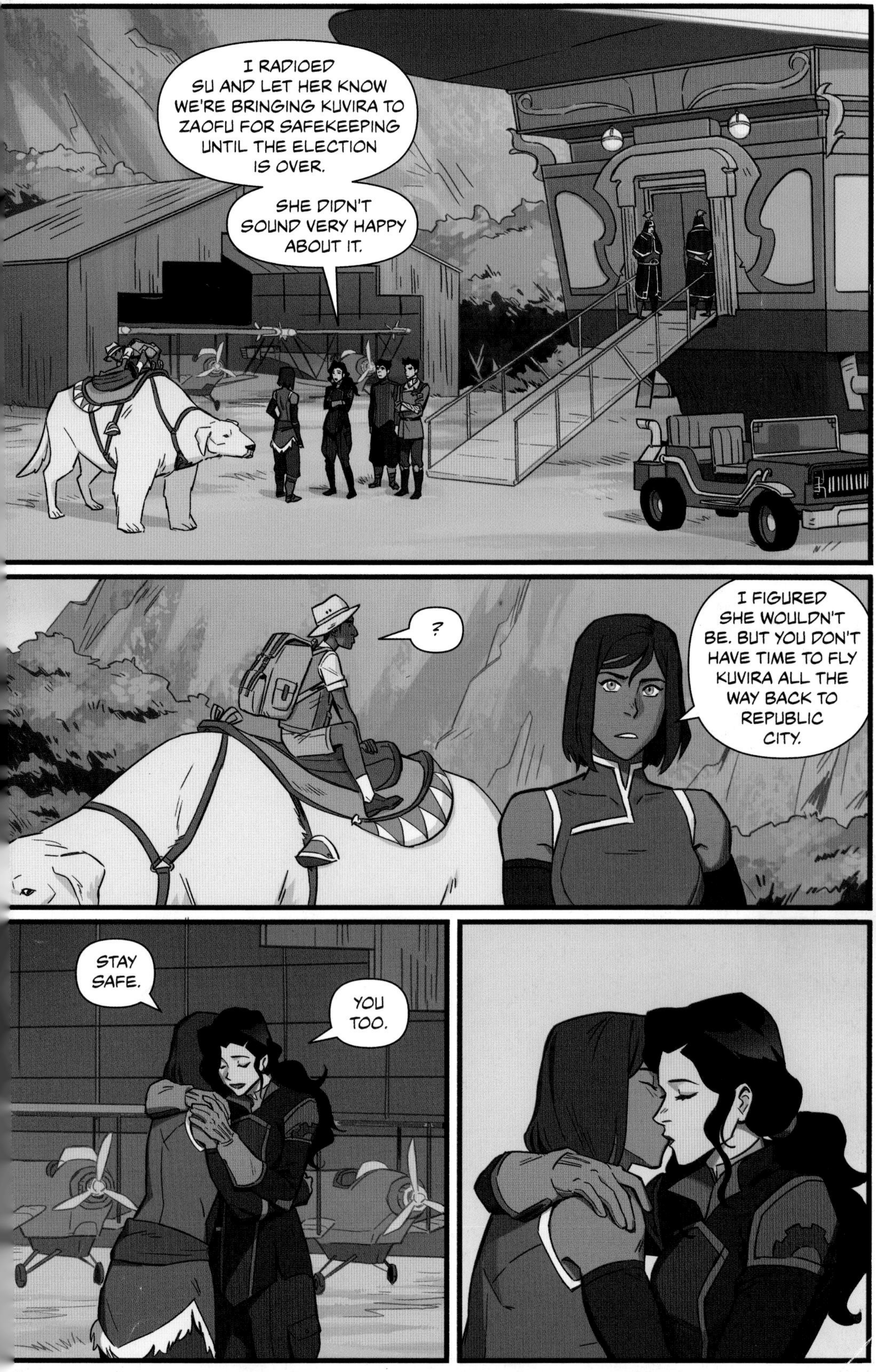
I RADIOED SU AND LET HER KNOW WE'RE BRINGING KUVIRA TO ZAOFU FOR SAFEKEEPING UNTIL THE ELECTION IS OVER.
SHE DIDN'T SOUND VERY HAPPY ABOUT IT.
?
I FIGURED SHE WOULDN'T BE. BUT YOU DON'T HAVE TIME TO FLY KUVIRA ALL THE WAY BACK TO REPUBLIC CITY.
STAY SAFE.
YOU TOO.

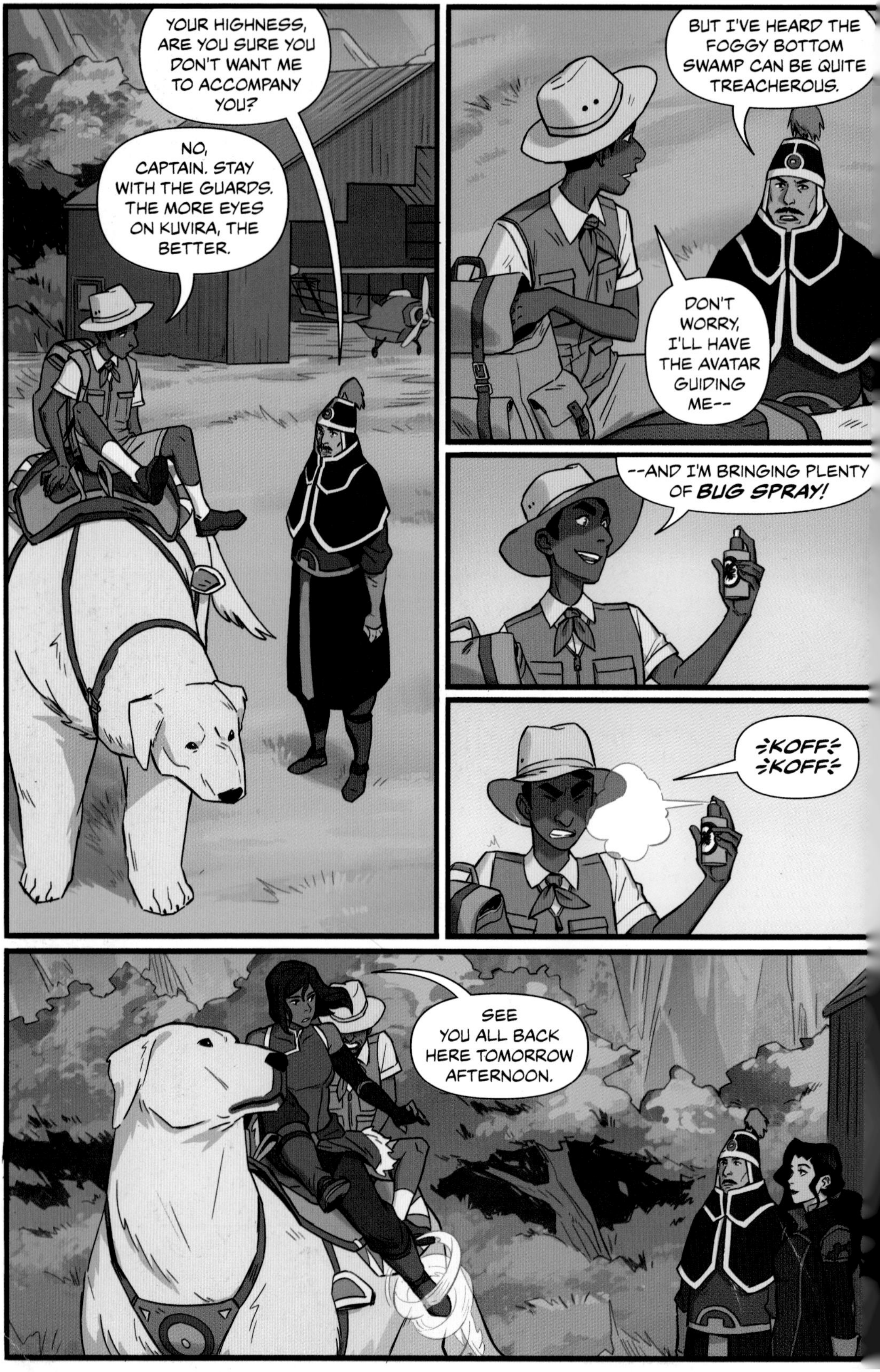
YOUR HIGHNESS, ARE YOU SURE YOU DON'T WANT ME TO ACCOMPANY YOU?
NO, CAPTAIN. STAY WITH THE GUARDS. THE MORE EYES ON KUVIRA, THE BETTER.
BUT I'VE HEARD THE FOGGY BOTTOM SWAMP CAN BE QUITE TREACHEROUS.
DON'T WORRY, I'LL HAVE THE AVATAR GUIDING ME--
--AND I'M BRINGING PLENTY OF **BUG SPRAY!**
KOFF KOFF
SEE YOU ALL BACK HERE TOMORROW AFTERNOON.

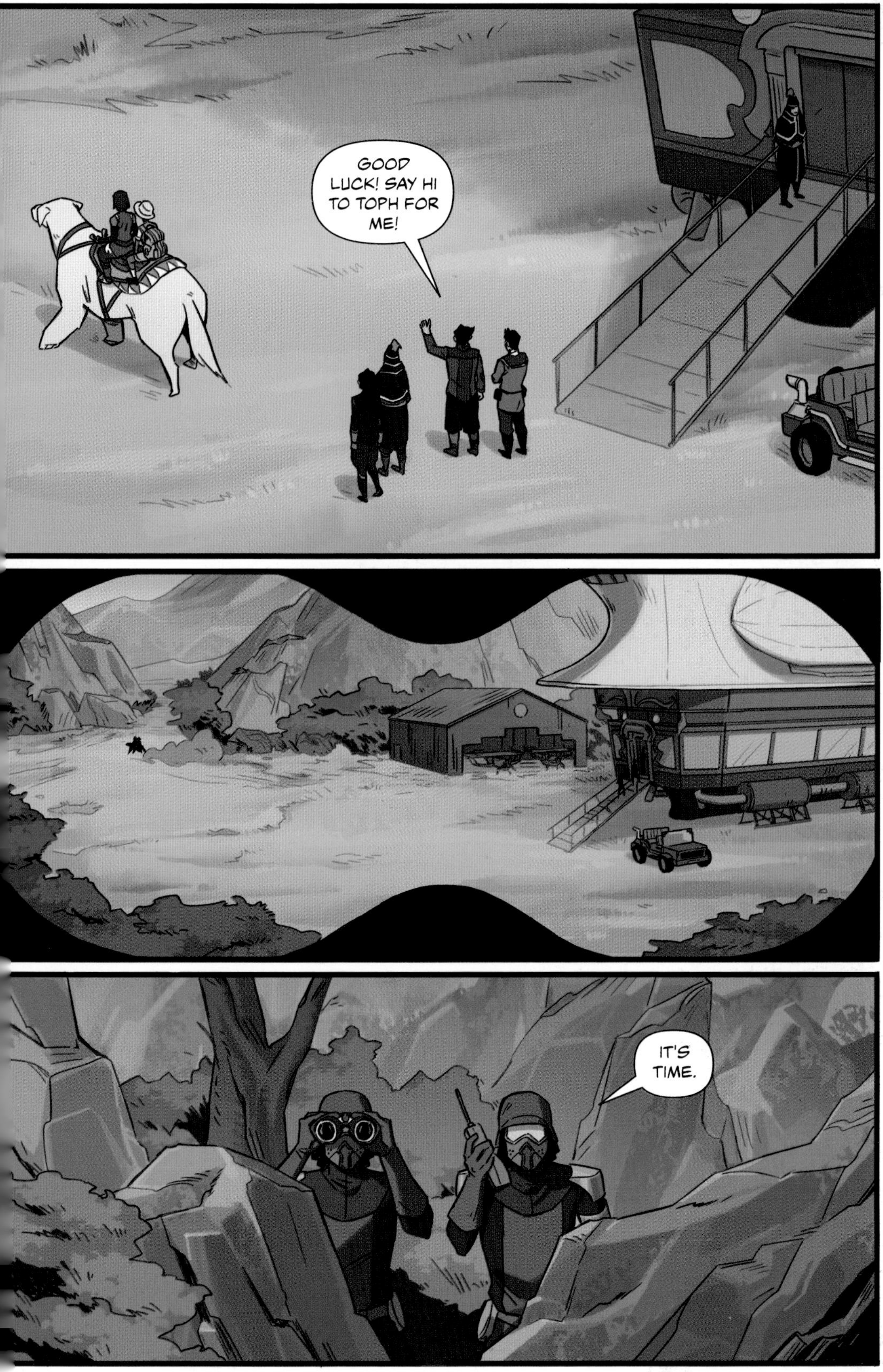
GOOD LUCK! SAY HI TO TOPH FOR ME!
IT'S TIME.

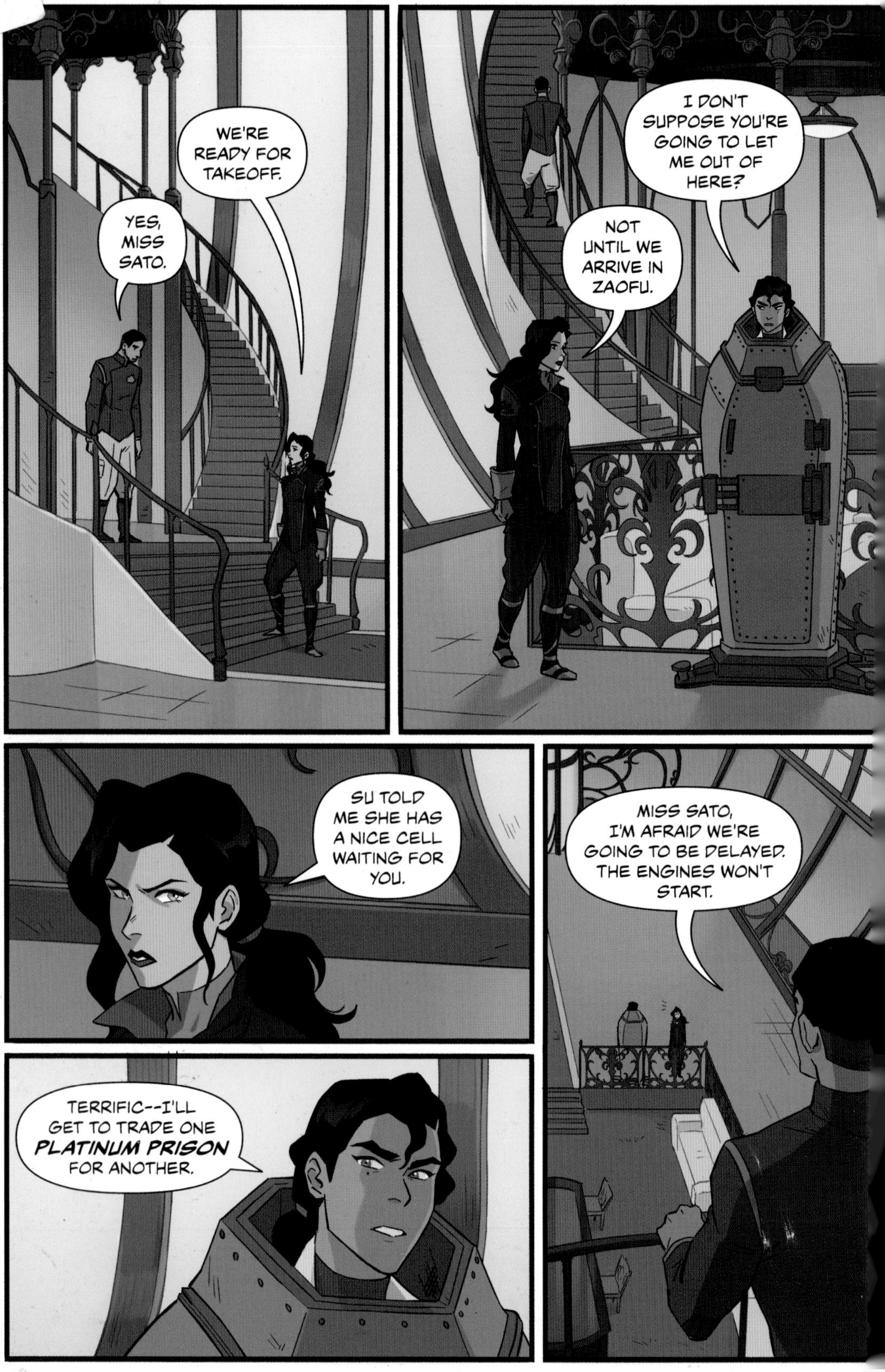
WE'RE READY FOR TAKEOFF.
YES, MISS SATO.
I DON'T SUPPOSE YOU'RE GOING TO LET ME OUT OF HERE?
NOT UNTIL WE ARRIVE IN ZAOFU.
SU TOLD ME SHE HAS A NICE CELL WAITING FOR YOU.
TERRIFIC--I'LL GET TO TRADE ONE PLATINUM PRISON FOR ANOTHER.
MISS SATO, I'M AFRAID WE'RE GOING TO BE DELAYED. THE ENGINES WON'T START.

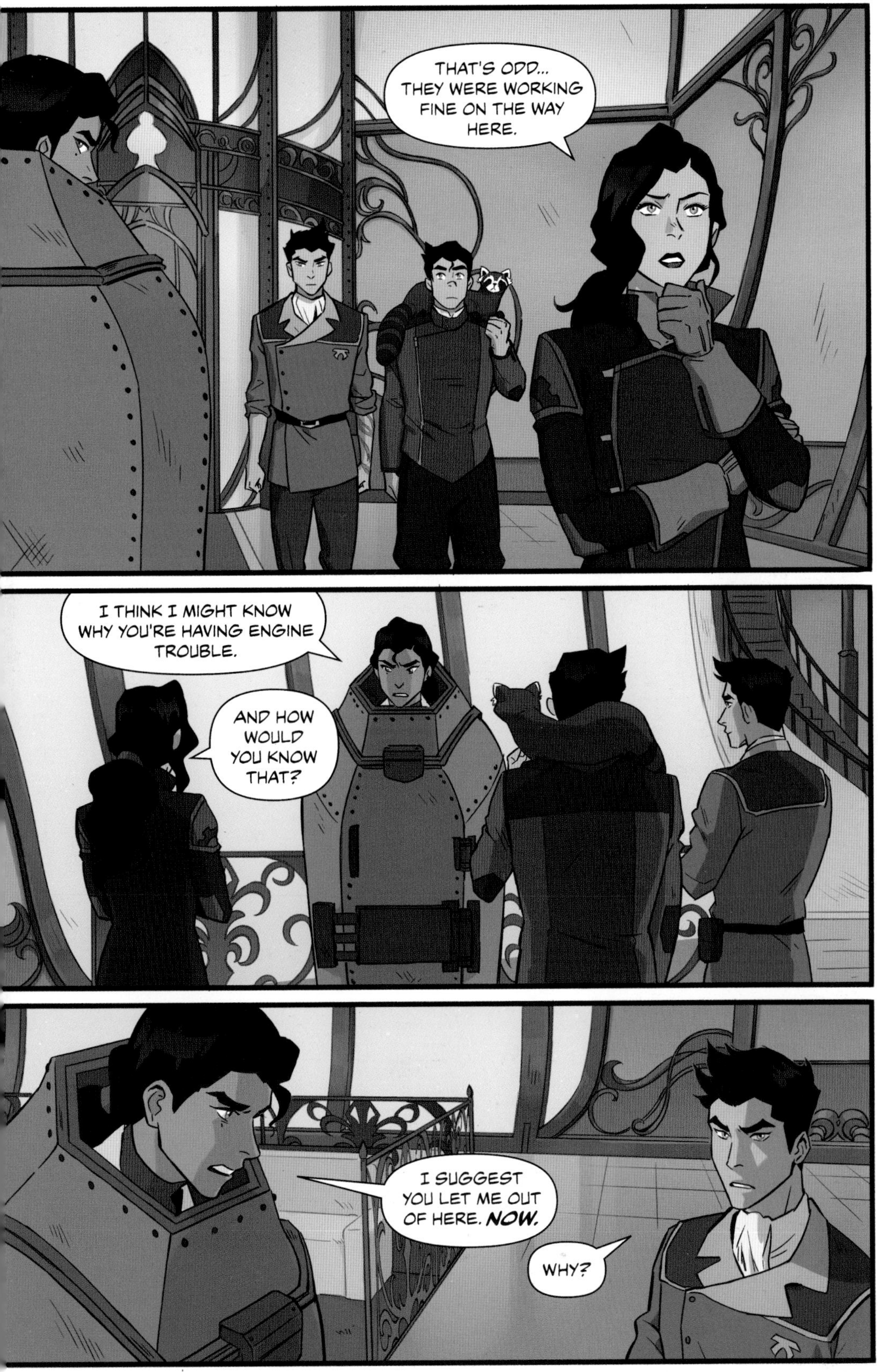
THAT'S ODD... THEY WERE WORKING FINE ON THE WAY HERE.
I THINK I MIGHT KNOW WHY YOU'RE HAVING ENGINE TROUBLE.
AND HOW WOULD YOU KNOW THAT?
I SUGGEST YOU LET ME OUT OF HERE. *NOW.*
WHY?

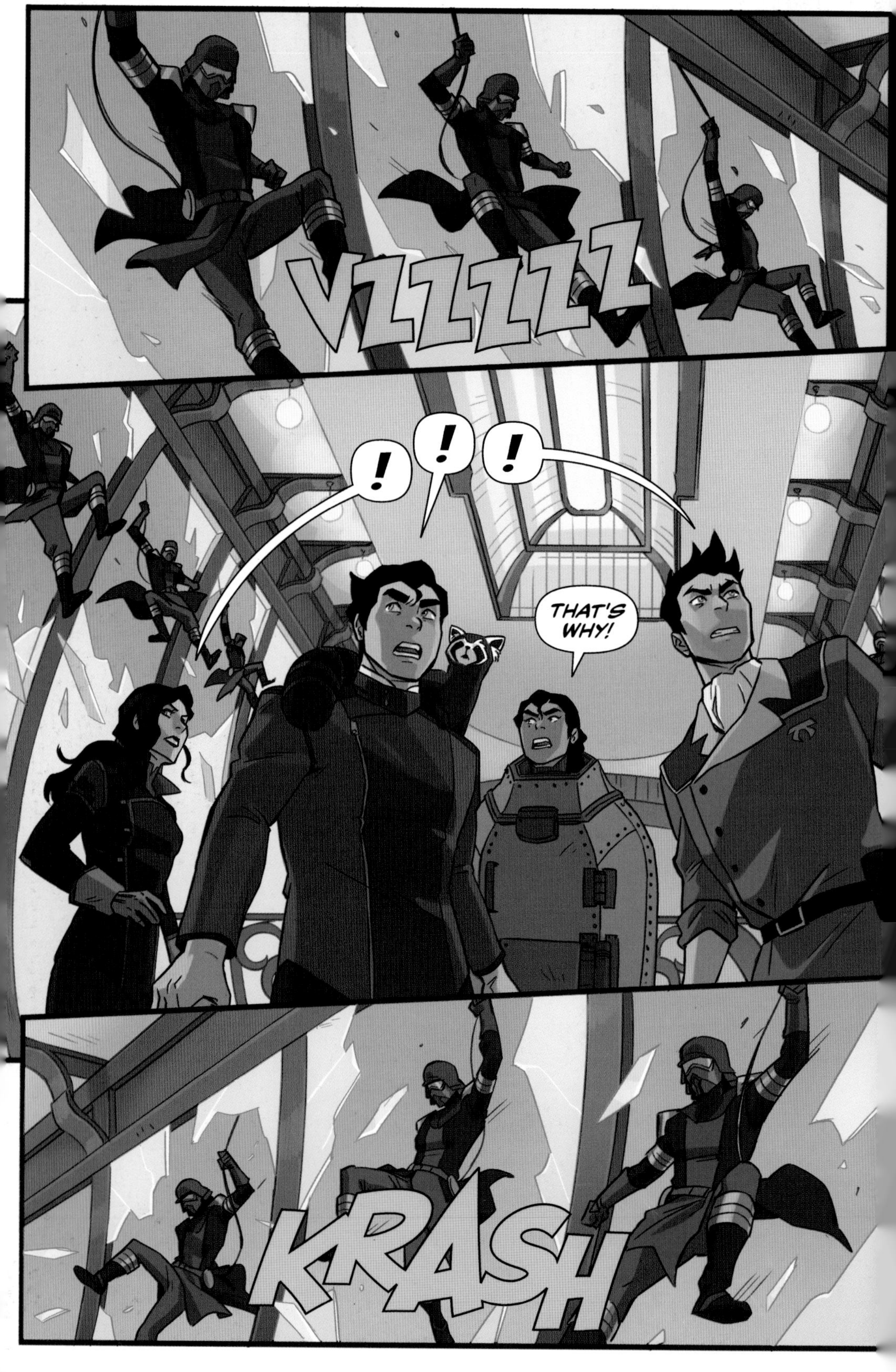
VZZZZZ
!
!
!
THAT'S WHY!
KRASH

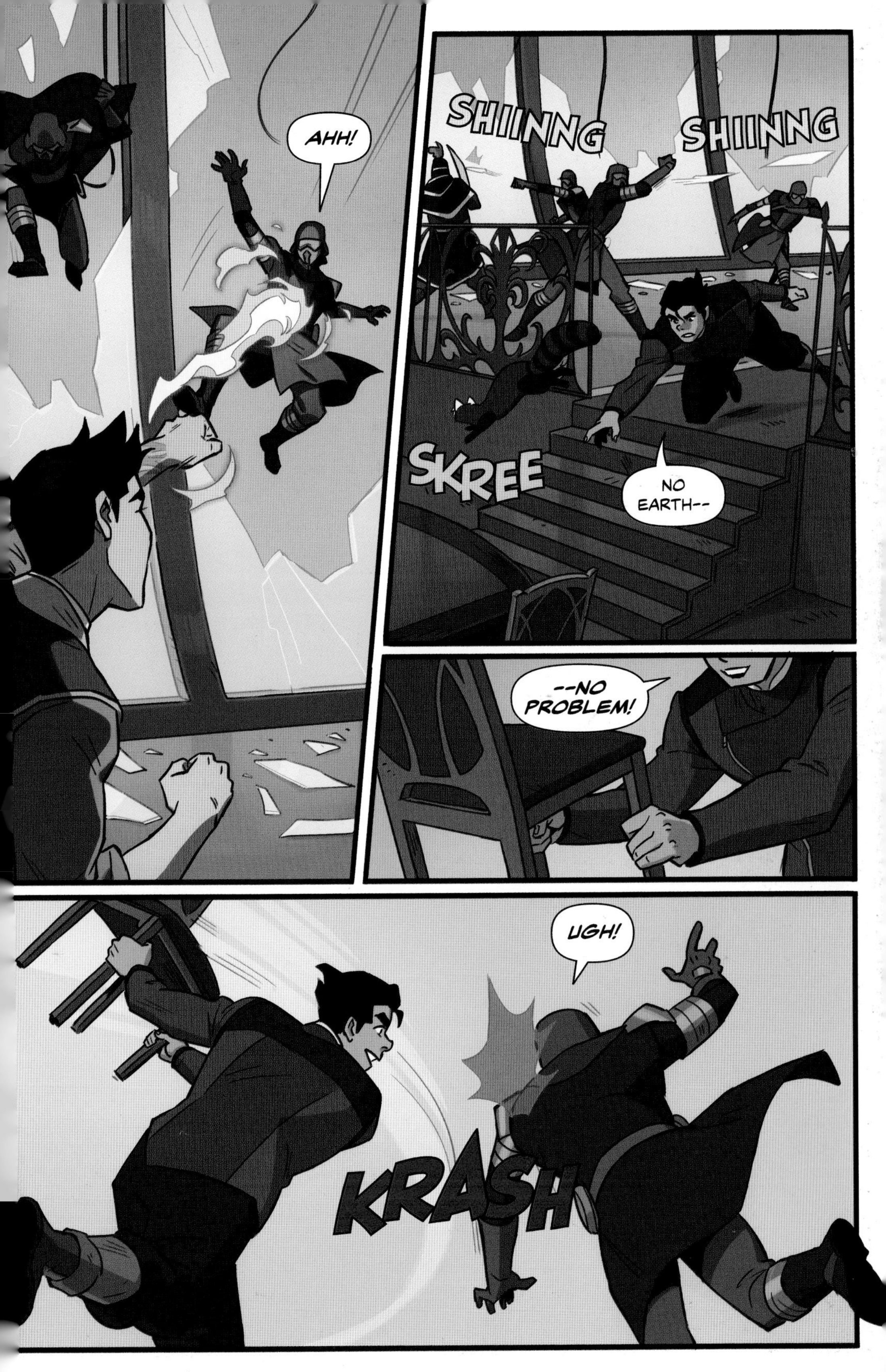
AHH!
SHIINNG
SHIINNG
SKREE
NO EARTH--
--NO PROBLEM!
UGH!
KRASH

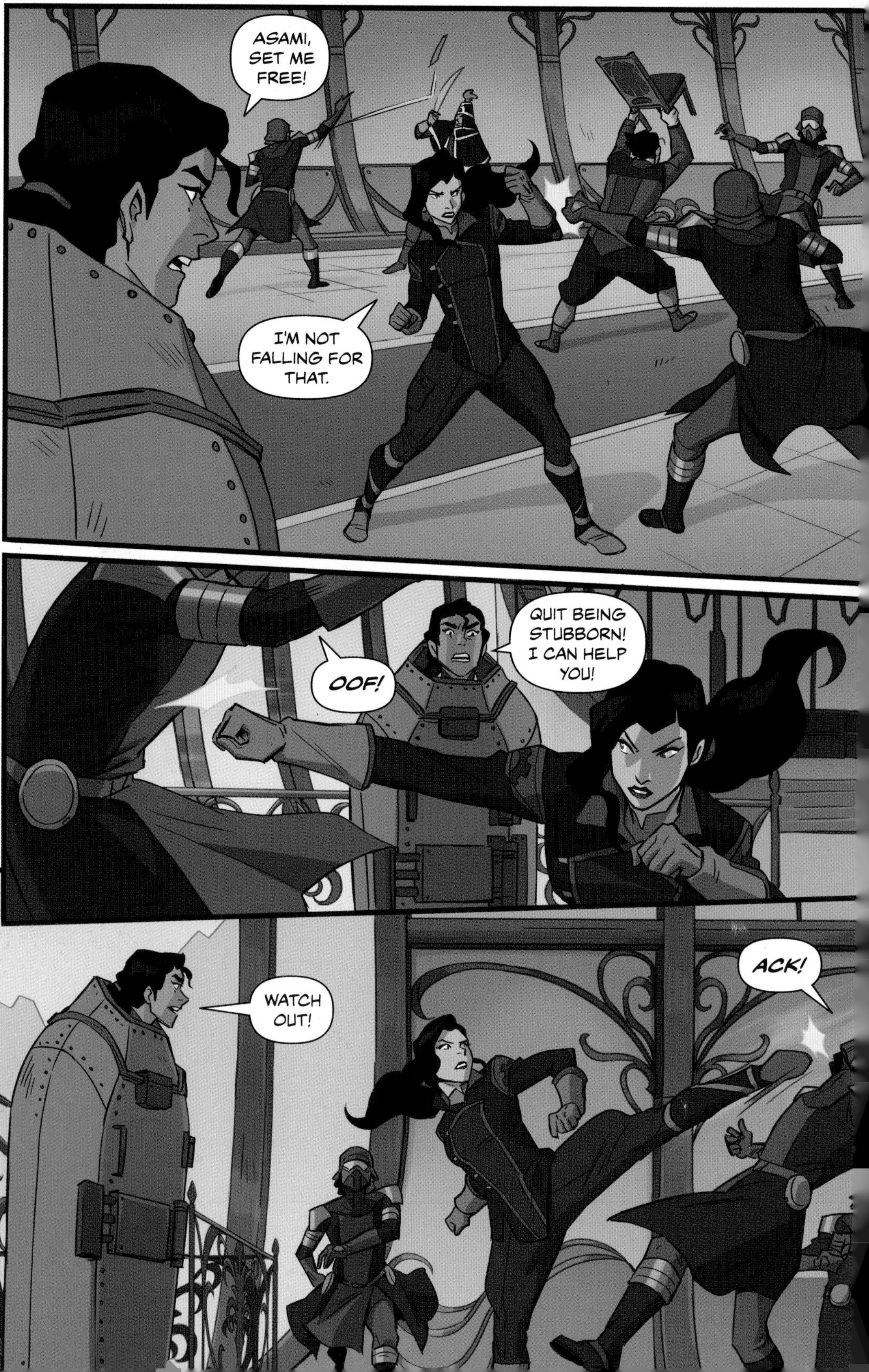
ASAMI, SET ME FREE!
I'M NOT FALLING FOR THAT.
QUIT BEING STUBBORN! I CAN HELP YOU!
OOF!
WATCH OUT!
ACK!

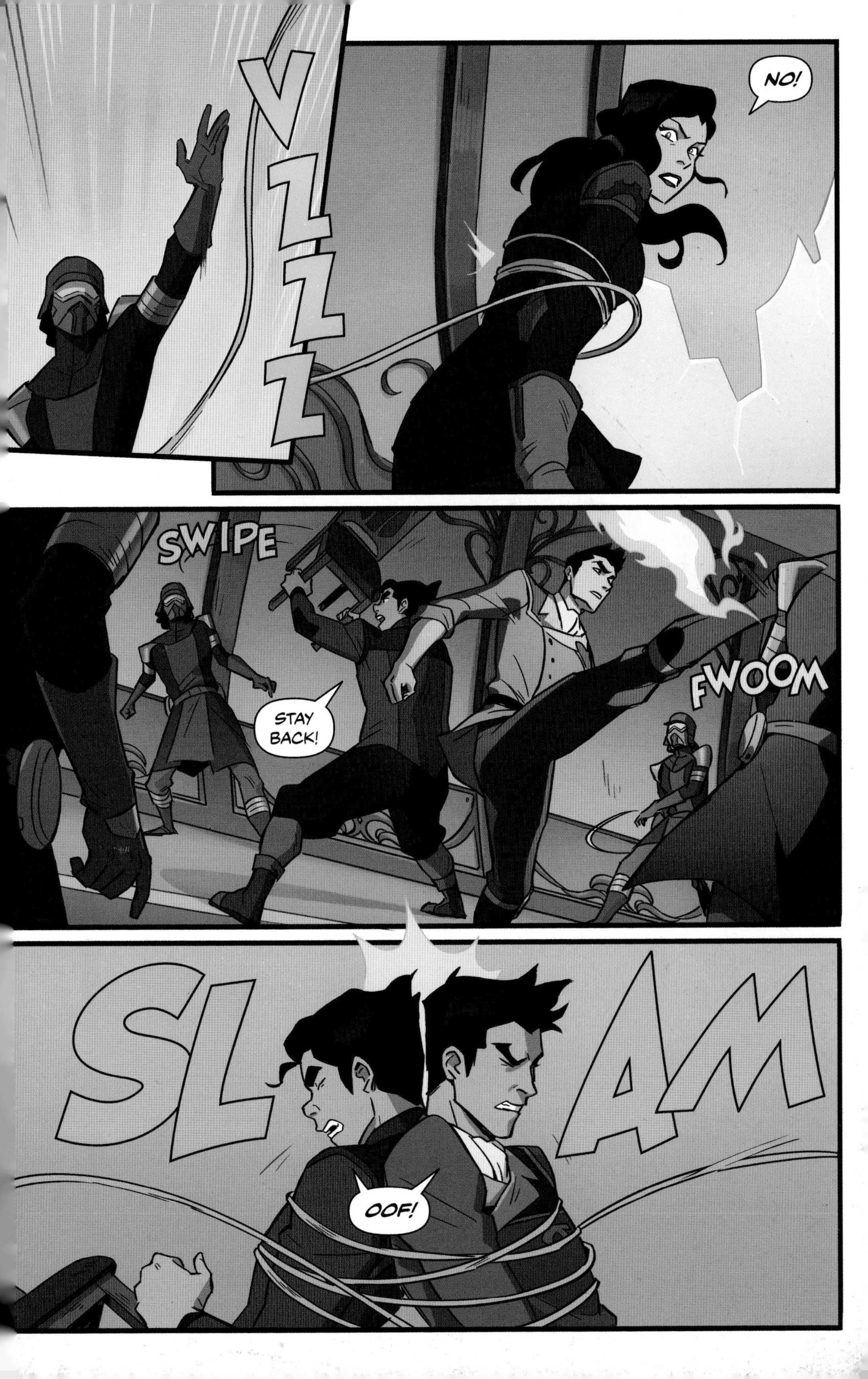
VZZZZ
NO!
SWIPE
STAY BACK!
FWOOM
SLAM
OOF!

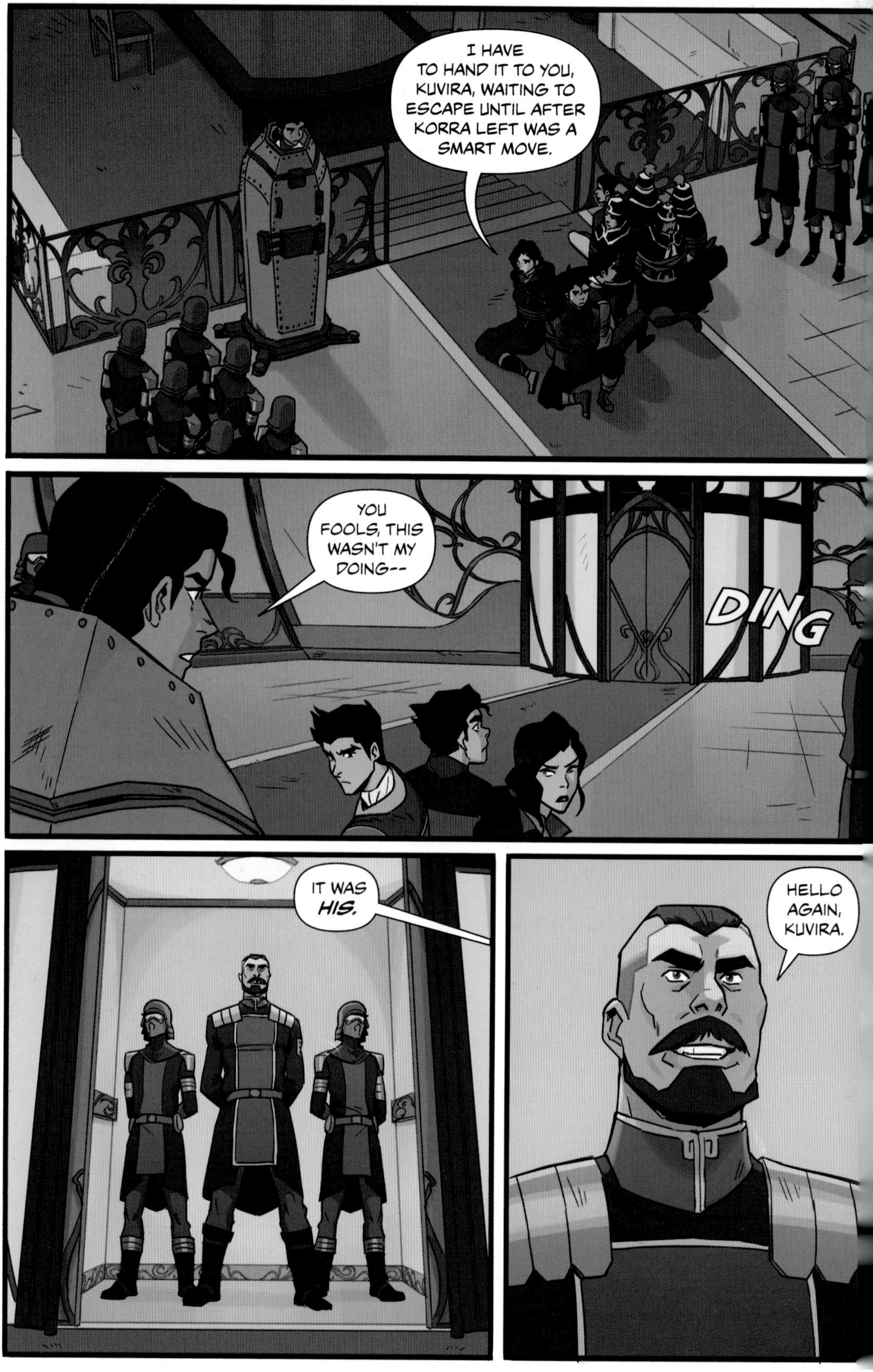
I HAVE TO HAND IT TO YOU, KUVIRA, WAITING TO ESCAPE UNTIL AFTER KORRA LEFT WAS A SMART MOVE.
YOU FOOLS, THIS WASN'T MY DOING--
DING
IT WAS *HIS.*
HELLO AGAIN, KUVIRA.

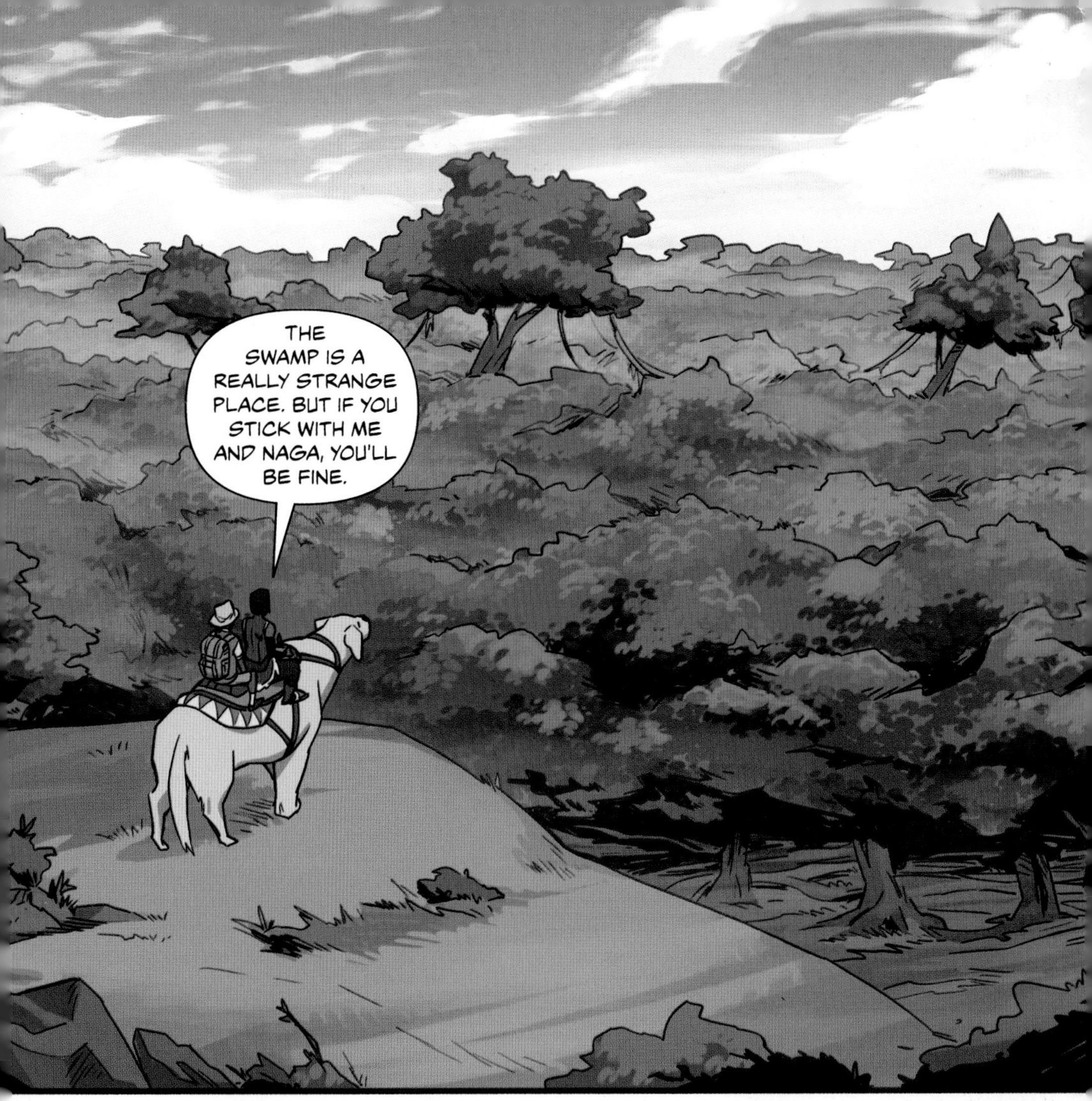
THE SWAMP IS A REALLY STRANGE PLACE. BUT IF YOU STICK WITH ME AND NAGA, YOU'LL BE FINE.

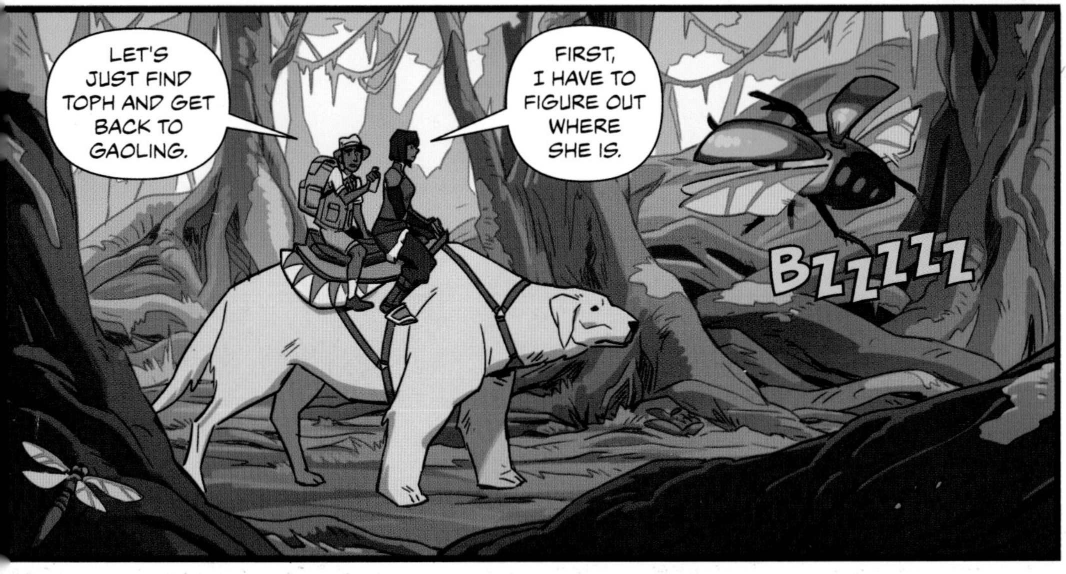
LET'S JUST FIND TOPH AND GET BACK TO GAOLING.
FIRST, I HAVE TO FIGURE OUT WHERE SHE IS.
BZZZZZ

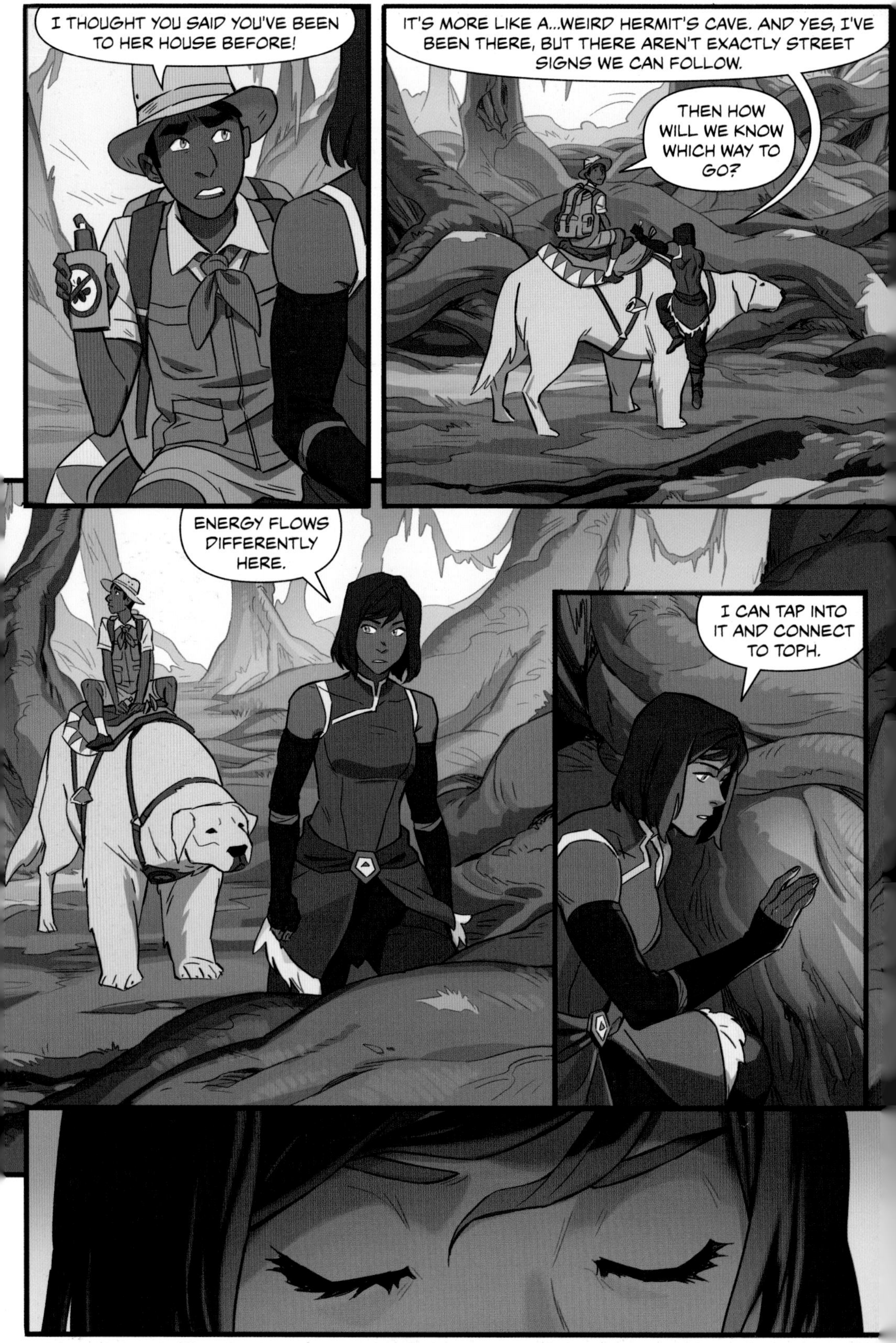
I THOUGHT YOU SAID YOU'VE BEEN TO HER HOUSE BEFORE!
IT'S MORE LIKE A...WEIRD HERMIT'S CAVE. AND YES, I'VE BEEN THERE, BUT THERE AREN'T EXACTLY STREET SIGNS WE CAN FOLLOW.
THEN HOW WILL WE KNOW WHICH WAY TO GO?
ENERGY FLOWS DIFFERENTLY HERE.
I CAN TAP INTO IT AND CONNECT TO TOPH.

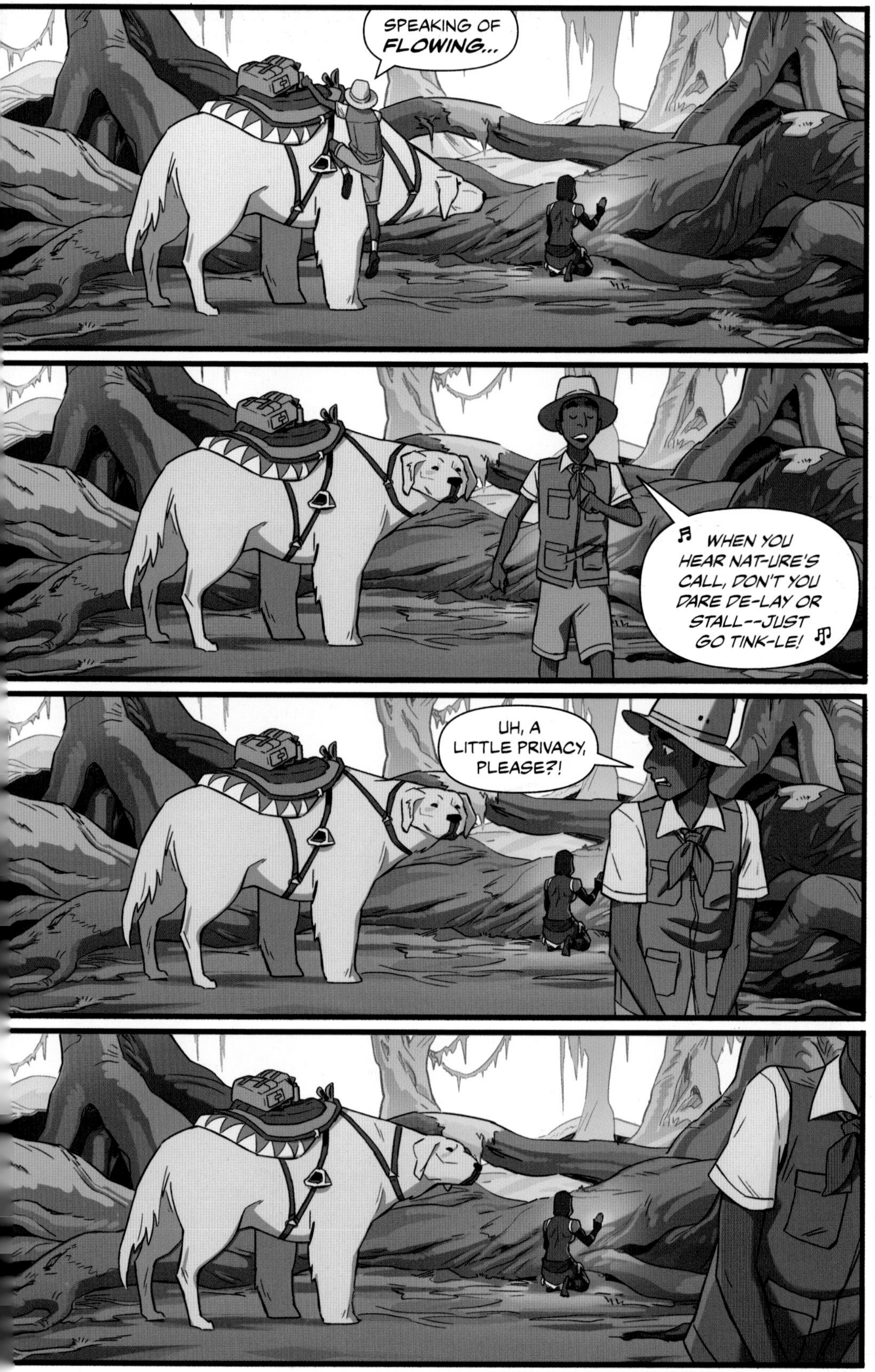
SPEAKING OF FLOWING...
♫ WHEN YOU HEAR NAT-URE'S CALL, DON'T YOU DARE DE-LAY OR STALL--JUST GO TINK-LE! ♫
UH, A LITTLE PRIVACY, PLEASE?!

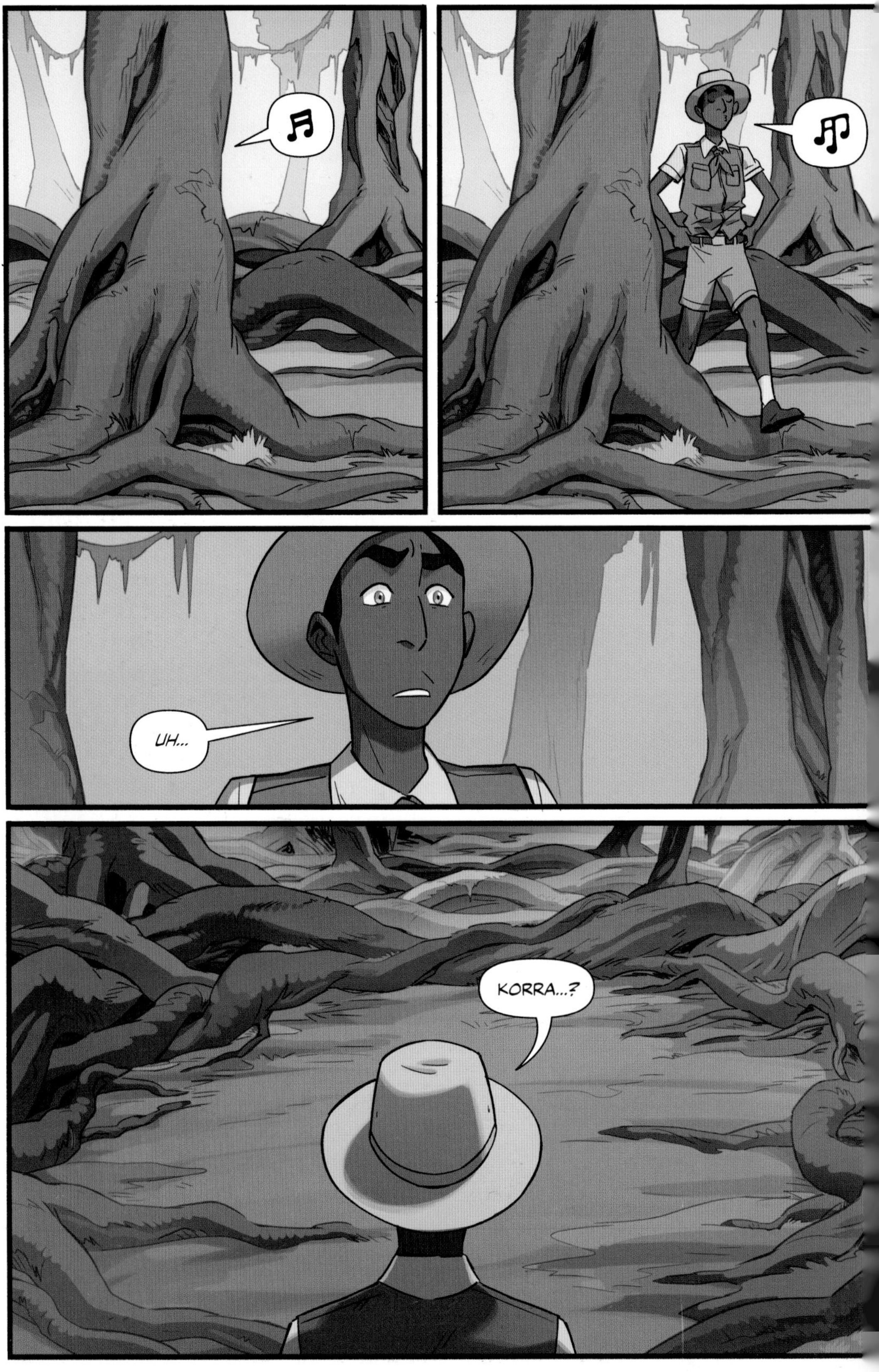

♬
♫
UH...
KORRA...?

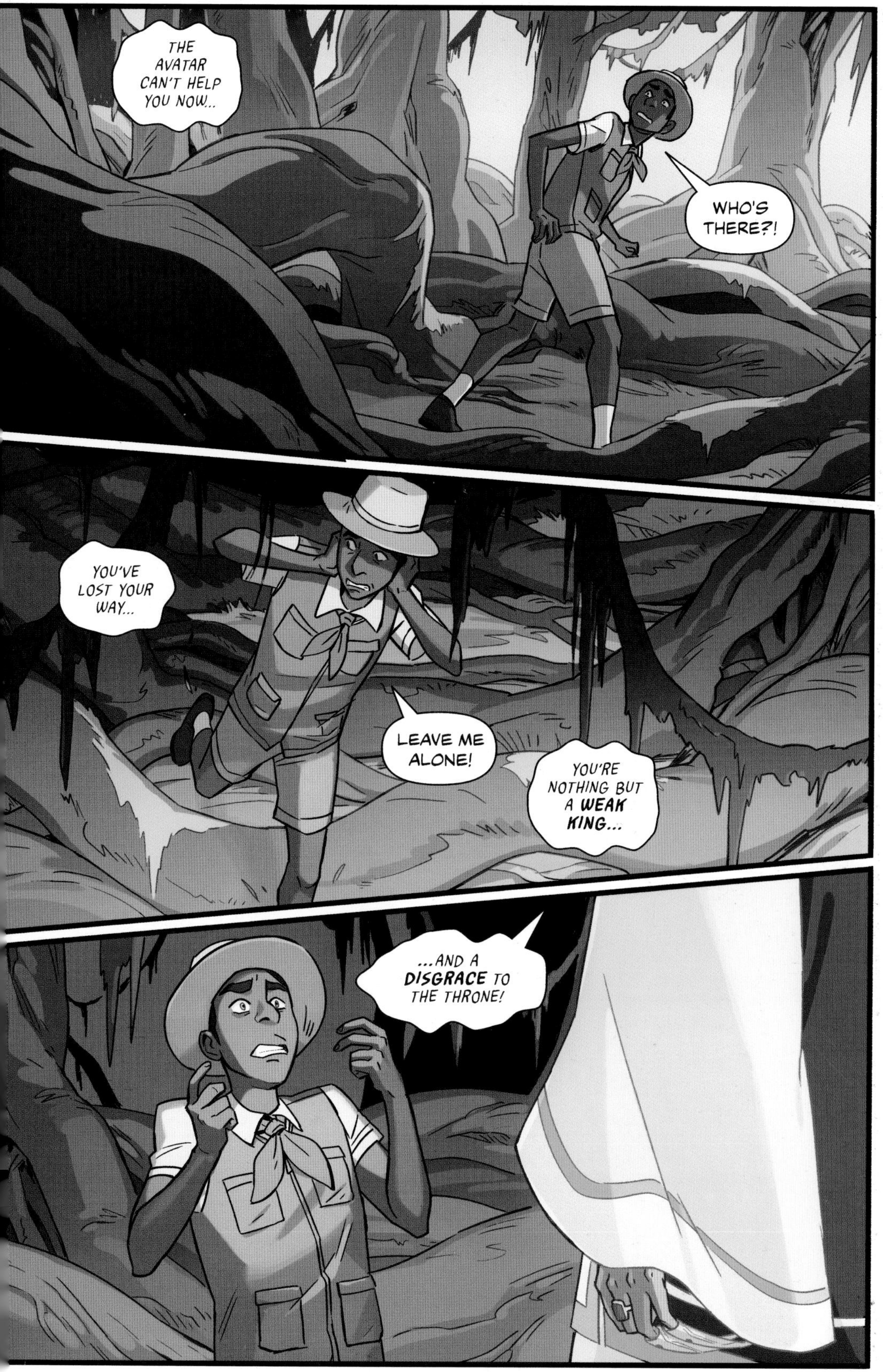

THE AVATAR CAN'T HELP YOU NOW...
WHO'S THERE?!
YOU'VE LOST YOUR WAY...
LEAVE ME ALONE!
YOU'RE NOTHING BUT A **WEAK KING...**
...AND A **DISGRACE** TO THE THRONE!

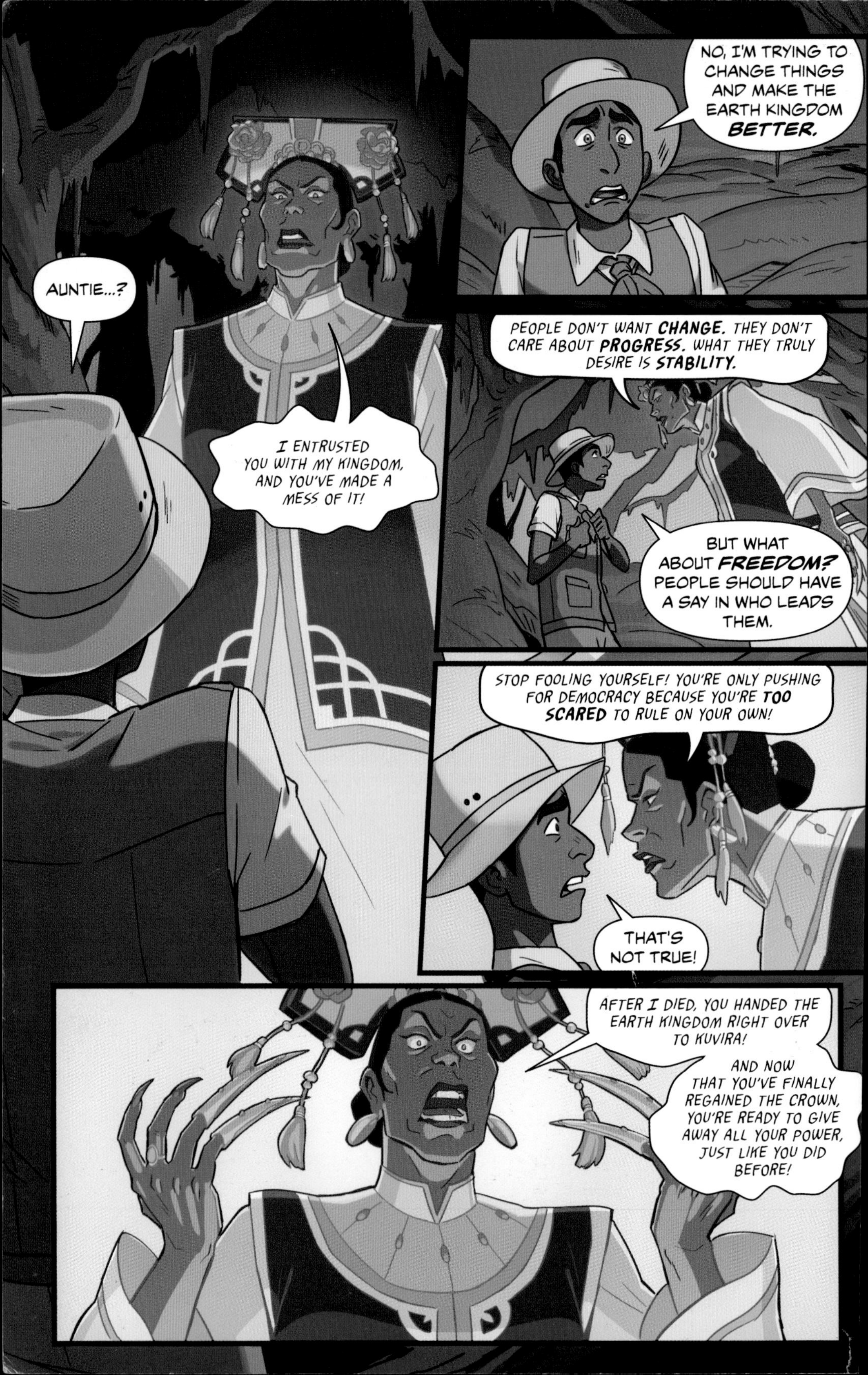
AUNTIE...?
I ENTRUSTED YOU WITH MY KINGDOM, AND YOU'VE MADE A MESS OF IT!
NO, I'M TRYING TO CHANGE THINGS AND MAKE THE EARTH KINGDOM BETTER.
PEOPLE DON'T WANT CHANGE. THEY DON'T CARE ABOUT PROGRESS. WHAT THEY TRULY DESIRE IS STABILITY.
BUT WHAT ABOUT FREEDOM? PEOPLE SHOULD HAVE A SAY IN WHO LEADS THEM.
STOP FOOLING YOURSELF! YOU'RE ONLY PUSHING FOR DEMOCRACY BECAUSE YOU'RE TOO SCARED TO RULE ON YOUR OWN!
THAT'S NOT TRUE!
AFTER I DIED, YOU HANDED THE EARTH KINGDOM RIGHT OVER TO KUVIRA!
AND NOW THAT YOU'VE FINALLY REGAINED THE CROWN, YOU'RE READY TO GIVE AWAY ALL YOUR POWER, JUST LIKE YOU DID BEFORE!

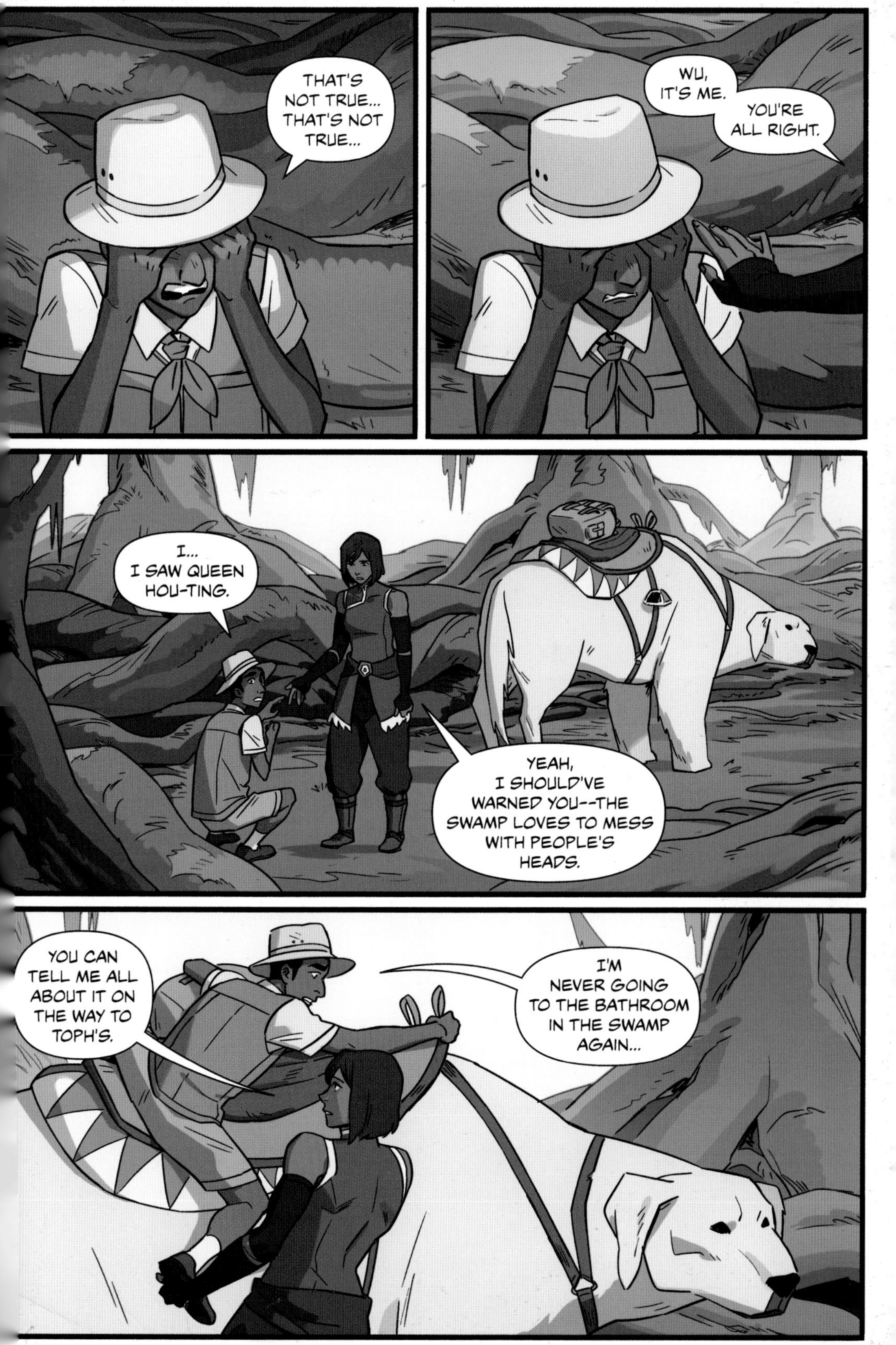

THAT'S NOT TRUE... THAT'S NOT TRUE...
WU, IT'S ME.
YOU'RE ALL RIGHT.
I... I SAW QUEEN HOU-TING.
YEAH, I SHOULD'VE WARNED YOU--THE SWAMP LOVES TO MESS WITH PEOPLE'S HEADS.
YOU CAN TELL ME ALL ABOUT IT ON THE WAY TO TOPH'S.
I'M NEVER GOING TO THE BATHROOM IN THE SWAMP AGAIN...

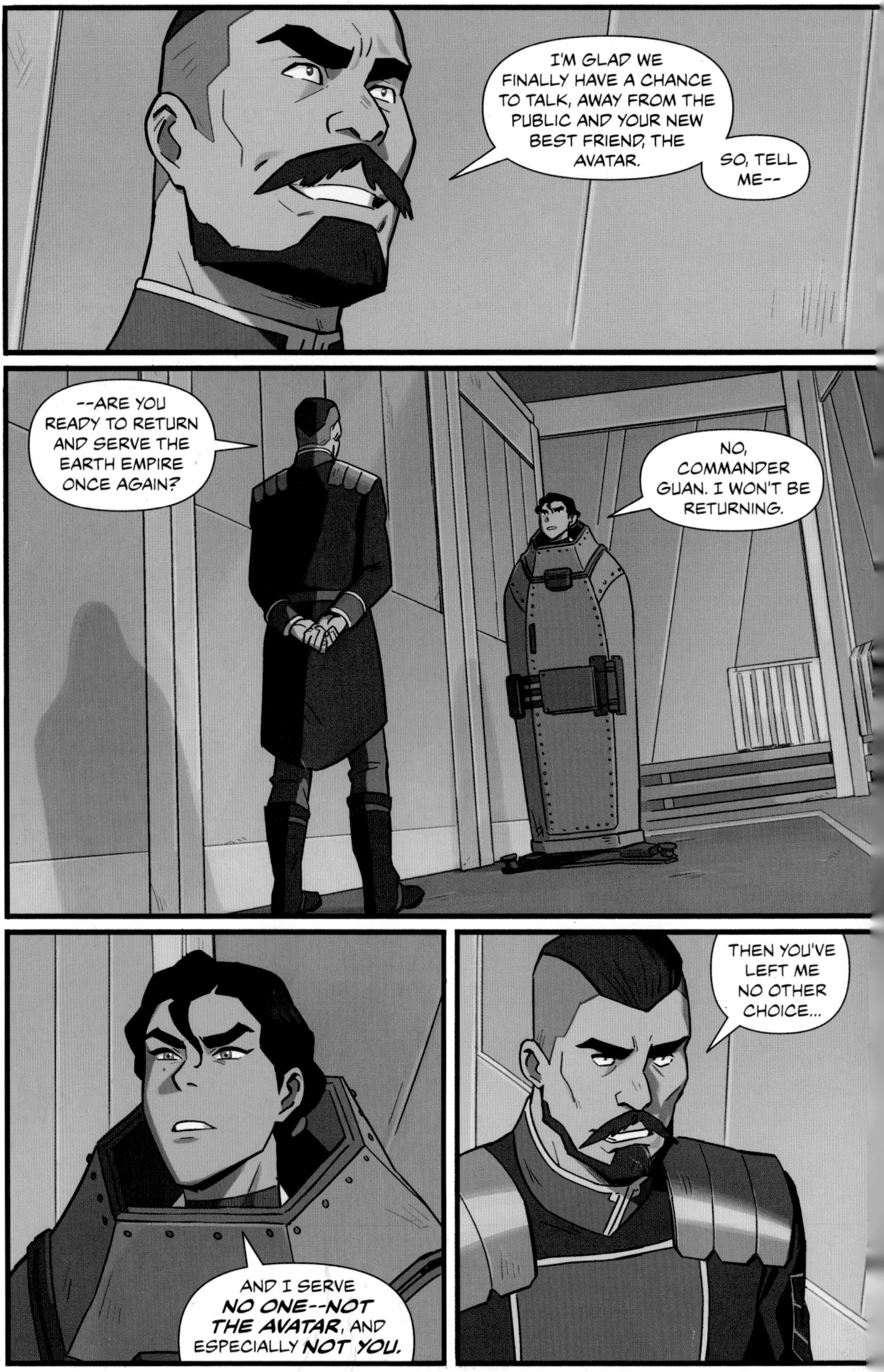

I'M GLAD WE FINALLY HAVE A CHANCE TO TALK, AWAY FROM THE PUBLIC AND YOUR NEW BEST FRIEND, THE AVATAR.
SO, TELL ME--
--ARE YOU READY TO RETURN AND SERVE THE EARTH EMPIRE ONCE AGAIN?
NO, COMMANDER GUAN. I WON'T BE RETURNING.
AND I SERVE NO ONE--NOT THE AVATAR, AND ESPECIALLY NOT YOU.
THEN YOU'VE LEFT ME NO OTHER CHOICE...

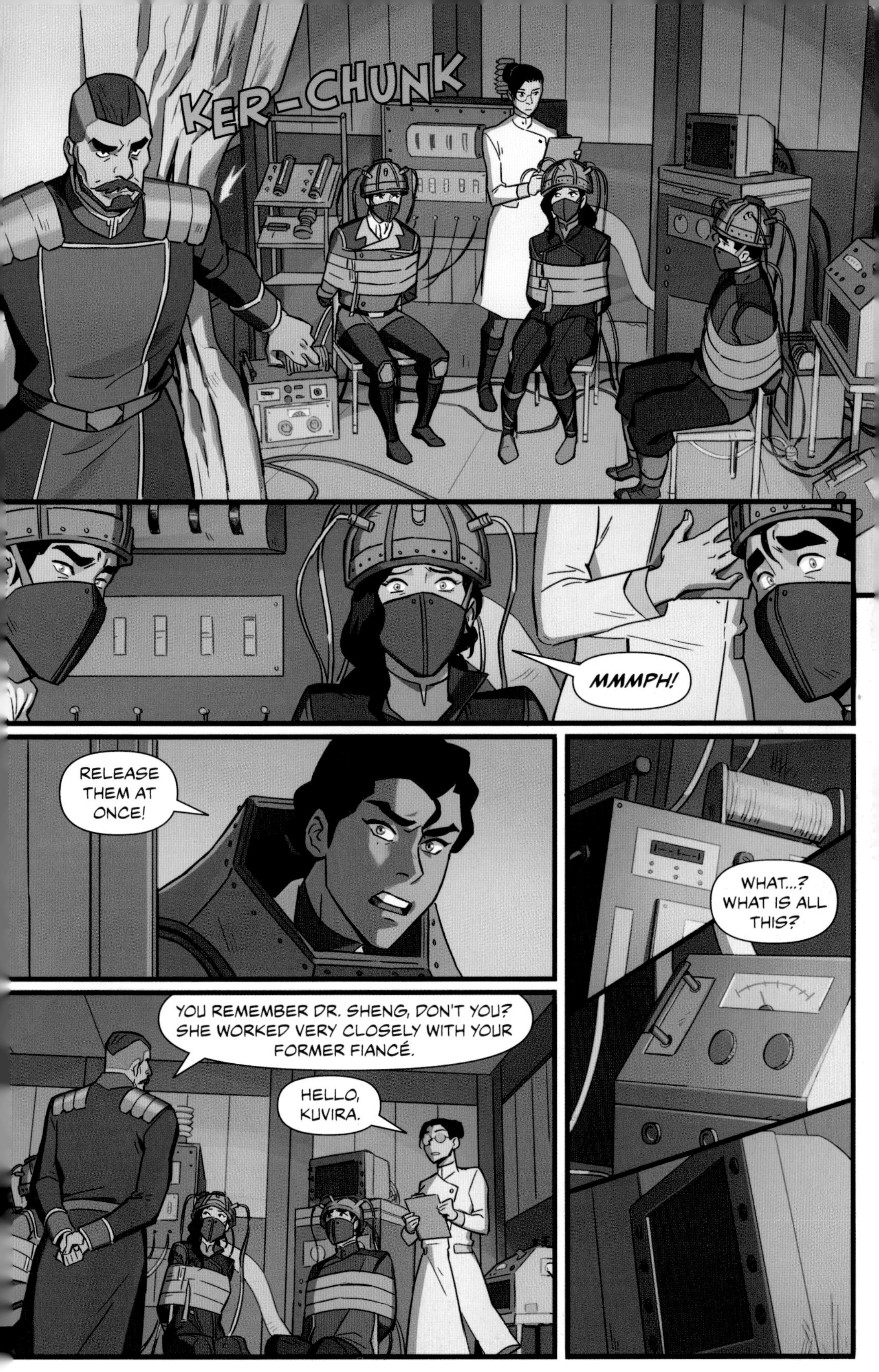
KER-CHUNK
MMMPH!
RELEASE THEM AT ONCE!
WHAT...? WHAT IS ALL THIS?
YOU REMEMBER DR. SHENG, DON'T YOU? SHE WORKED VERY CLOSELY WITH YOUR FORMER FIANCÉ.
HELLO, KUVIRA.

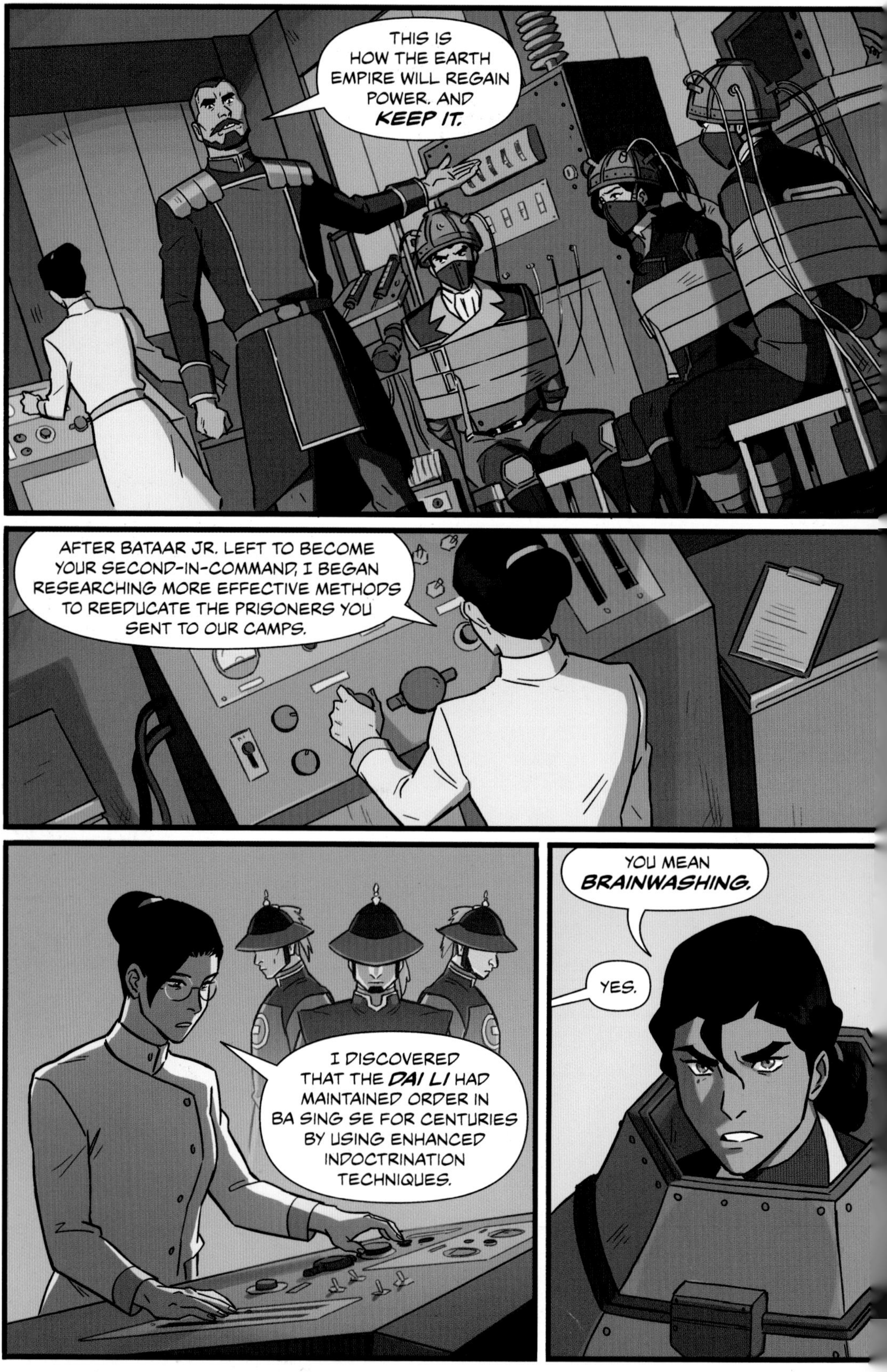
THIS IS HOW THE EARTH EMPIRE WILL REGAIN POWER. AND *KEEP IT.*
AFTER BATAAR JR. LEFT TO BECOME YOUR SECOND-IN-COMMAND, I BEGAN RESEARCHING MORE EFFECTIVE METHODS TO REEDUCATE THE PRISONERS YOU SENT TO OUR CAMPS.
I DISCOVERED THAT THE *DAI LI* HAD MAINTAINED ORDER IN BA SING SE FOR CENTURIES BY USING ENHANCED INDOCTRINATION TECHNIQUES.
YOU MEAN *BRAINWASHING.*
YES.

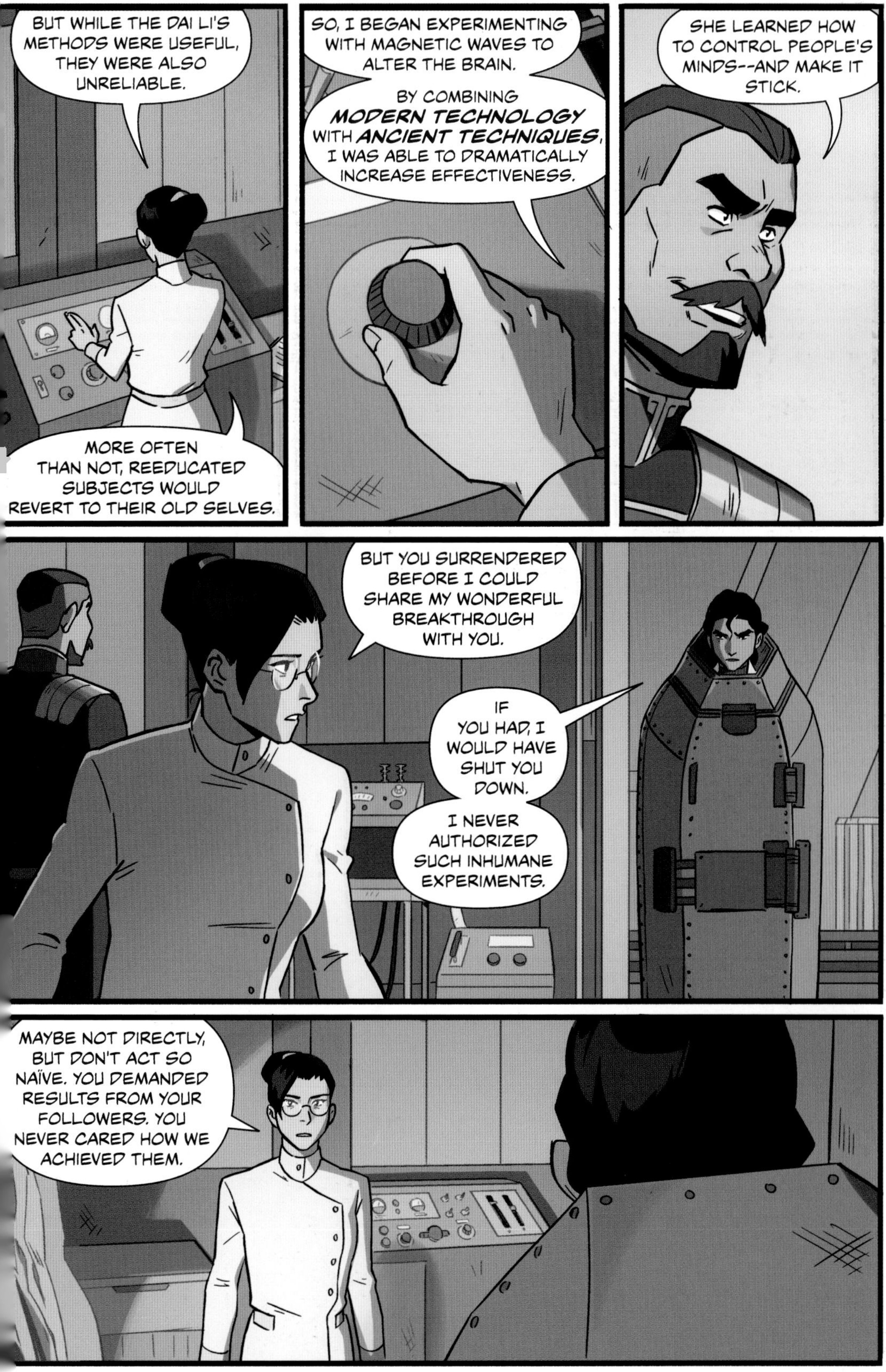
BUT WHILE THE DAI LI'S METHODS WERE USEFUL, THEY WERE ALSO UNRELIABLE.
MORE OFTEN THAN NOT, REEDUCATED SUBJECTS WOULD REVERT TO THEIR OLD SELVES.
SO, I BEGAN EXPERIMENTING WITH MAGNETIC WAVES TO ALTER THE BRAIN.
BY COMBINING **MODERN TECHNOLOGY** WITH **ANCIENT TECHNIQUES**, I WAS ABLE TO DRAMATICALLY INCREASE EFFECTIVENESS.
SHE LEARNED HOW TO CONTROL PEOPLE'S MINDS--AND MAKE IT STICK.
BUT YOU SURRENDERED BEFORE I COULD SHARE MY WONDERFUL BREAKTHROUGH WITH YOU.
IF YOU HAD, I WOULD HAVE SHUT YOU DOWN.
I NEVER AUTHORIZED SUCH INHUMANE EXPERIMENTS.
MAYBE NOT DIRECTLY, BUT DON'T ACT SO NAÏVE. YOU DEMANDED RESULTS FROM YOUR FOLLOWERS. YOU NEVER CARED HOW WE ACHIEVED THEM.

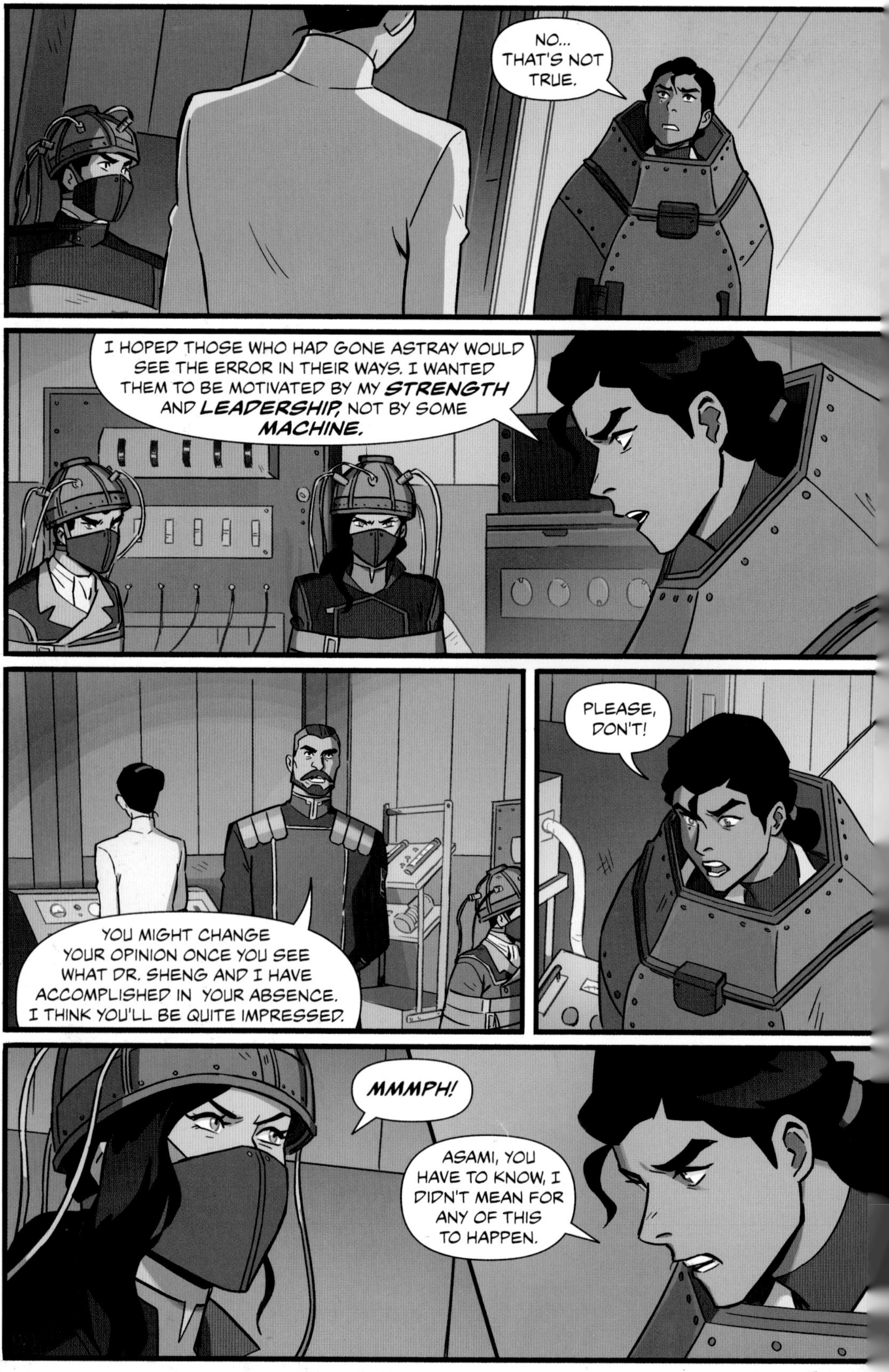
NO... THAT'S NOT TRUE.
I HOPED THOSE WHO HAD GONE ASTRAY WOULD SEE THE ERROR IN THEIR WAYS. I WANTED THEM TO BE MOTIVATED BY MY STRENGTH AND LEADERSHIP, NOT BY SOME MACHINE.
YOU MIGHT CHANGE YOUR OPINION ONCE YOU SEE WHAT DR. SHENG AND I HAVE ACCOMPLISHED IN YOUR ABSENCE. I THINK YOU'LL BE QUITE IMPRESSED.
PLEASE, DON'T!
MMMPH!
ASAMI, YOU HAVE TO KNOW, I DIDN'T MEAN FOR ANY OF THIS TO HAPPEN.

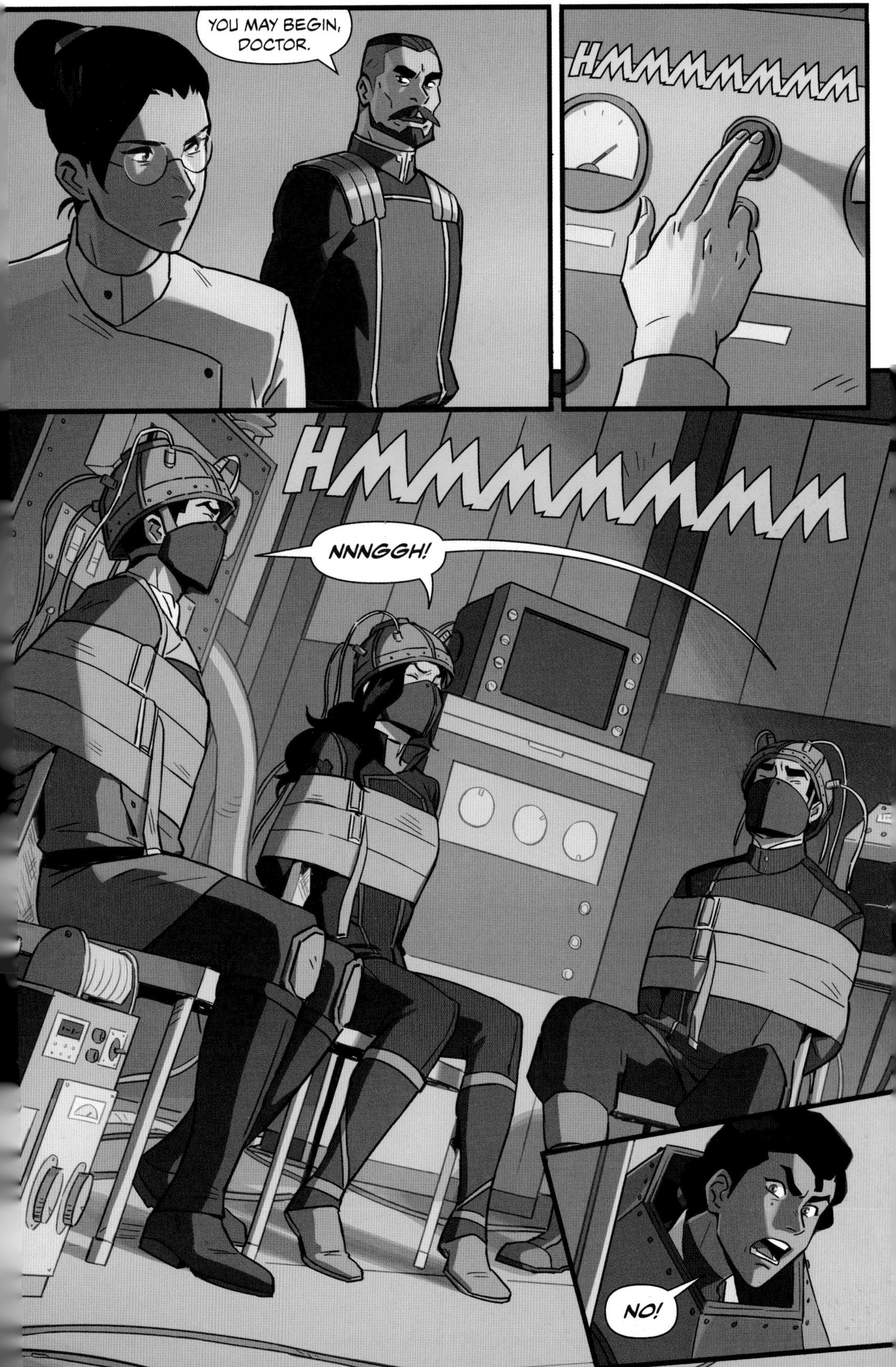
YOU MAY BEGIN, DOCTOR.
HMMMMMMMMM
HMMMMMMMMM
NNNGGH!
NO!

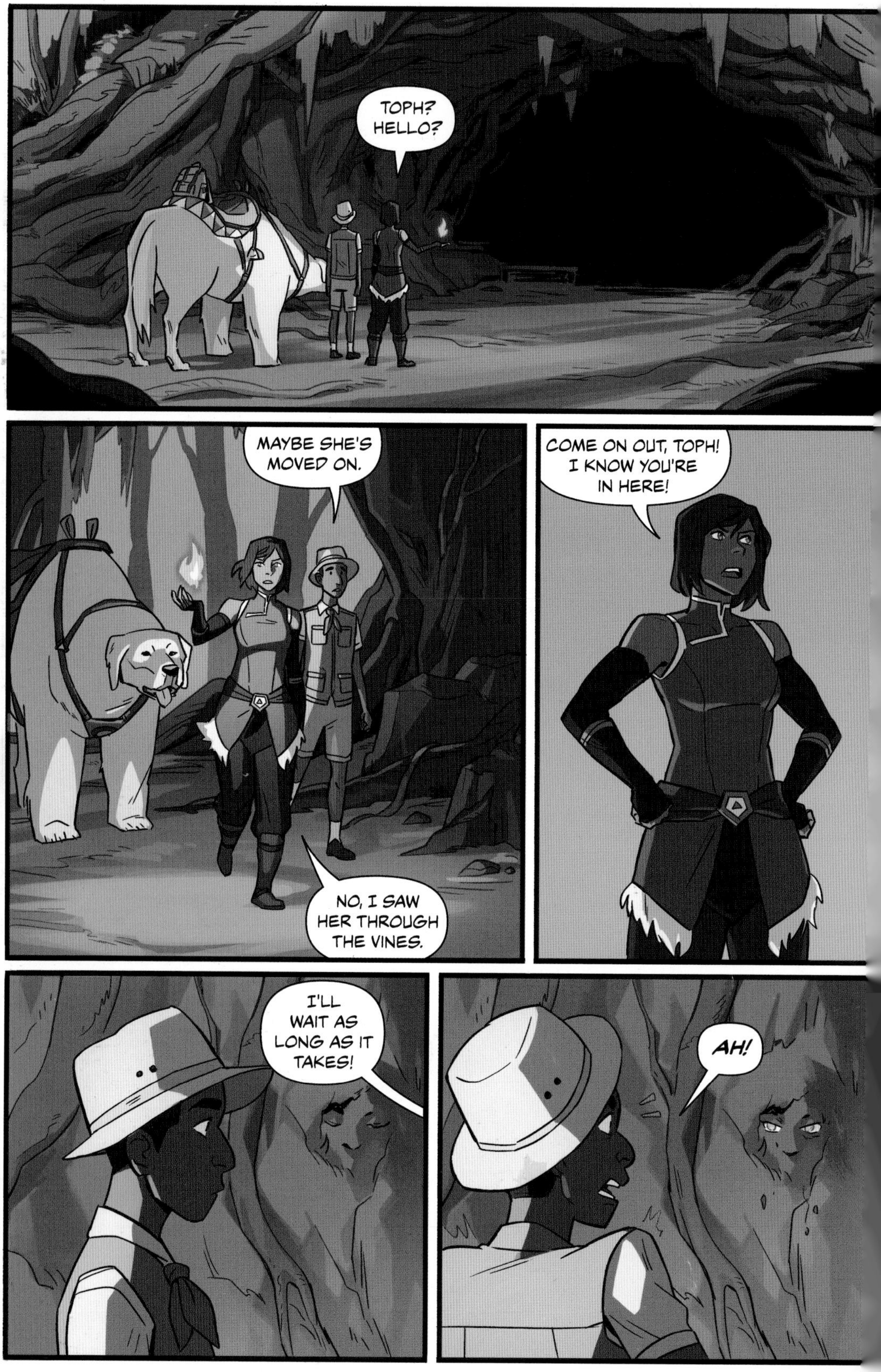
TOPH? HELLO?
MAYBE SHE'S MOVED ON.
NO, I SAW HER THROUGH THE VINES.
COME ON OUT, TOPH! I KNOW YOU'RE IN HERE!
I'LL WAIT AS LONG AS IT TAKES!
AH!

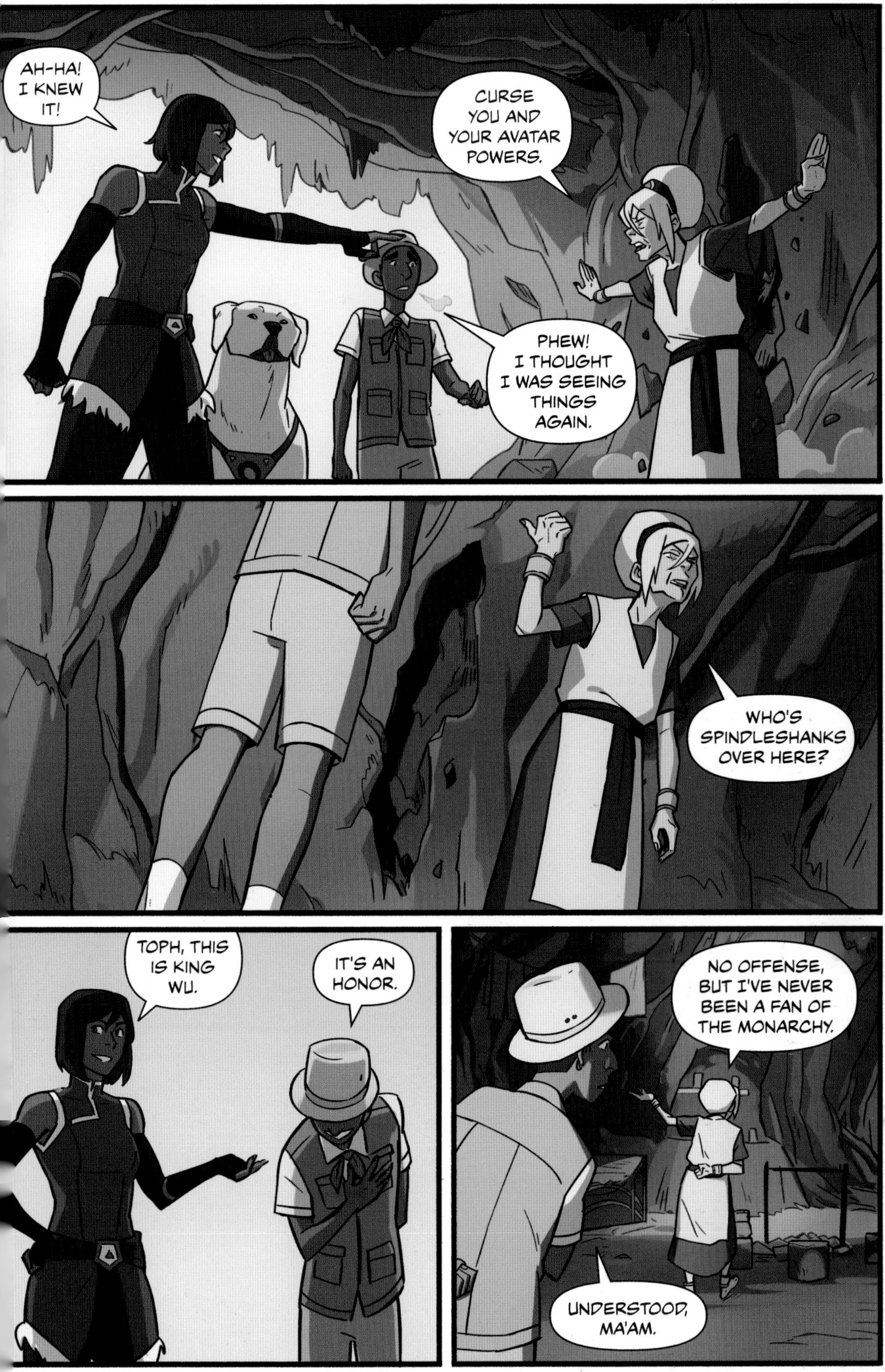
AH-HA! I KNEW IT!
CURSE YOU AND YOUR AVATAR POWERS.
PHEW! I THOUGHT I WAS SEEING THINGS AGAIN.
WHO'S SPINDLESHANKS OVER HERE?
TOPH, THIS IS KING WU.
IT'S AN HONOR.
NO OFFENSE, BUT I'VE NEVER BEEN A FAN OF THE MONARCHY.
UNDERSTOOD, MA'AM.

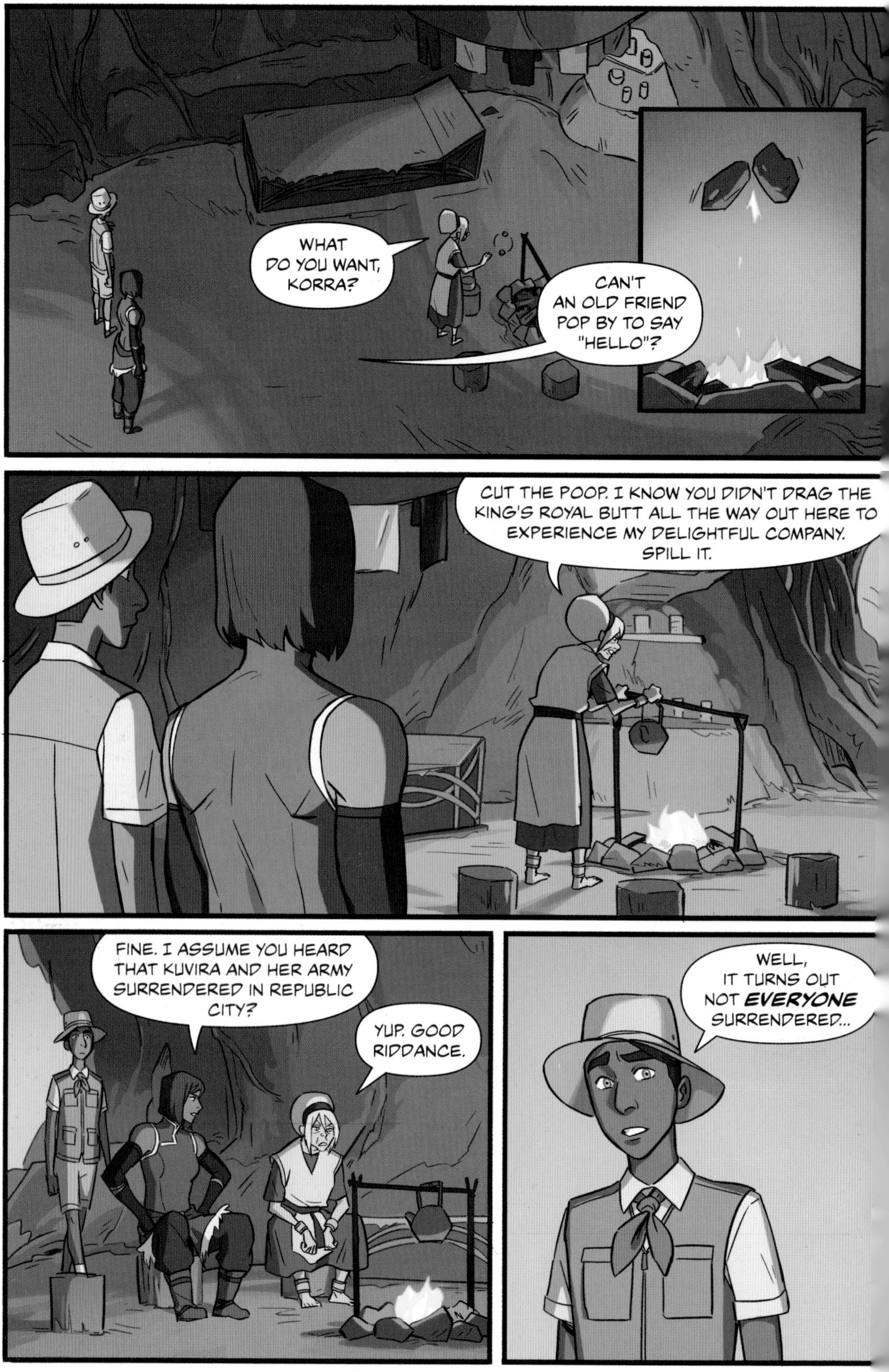
WHAT DO YOU WANT, KORRA?
CAN'T AN OLD FRIEND POP BY TO SAY "HELLO"?
CUT THE POOP. I KNOW YOU DIDN'T DRAG THE KING'S ROYAL BUTT ALL THE WAY OUT HERE TO EXPERIENCE MY DELIGHTFUL COMPANY. SPILL IT.
FINE. I ASSUME YOU HEARD THAT KUVIRA AND HER ARMY SURRENDERED IN REPUBLIC CITY?
YUP. GOOD RIDDANCE.
WELL, IT TURNS OUT NOT ***EVERYONE*** SURRENDERED...

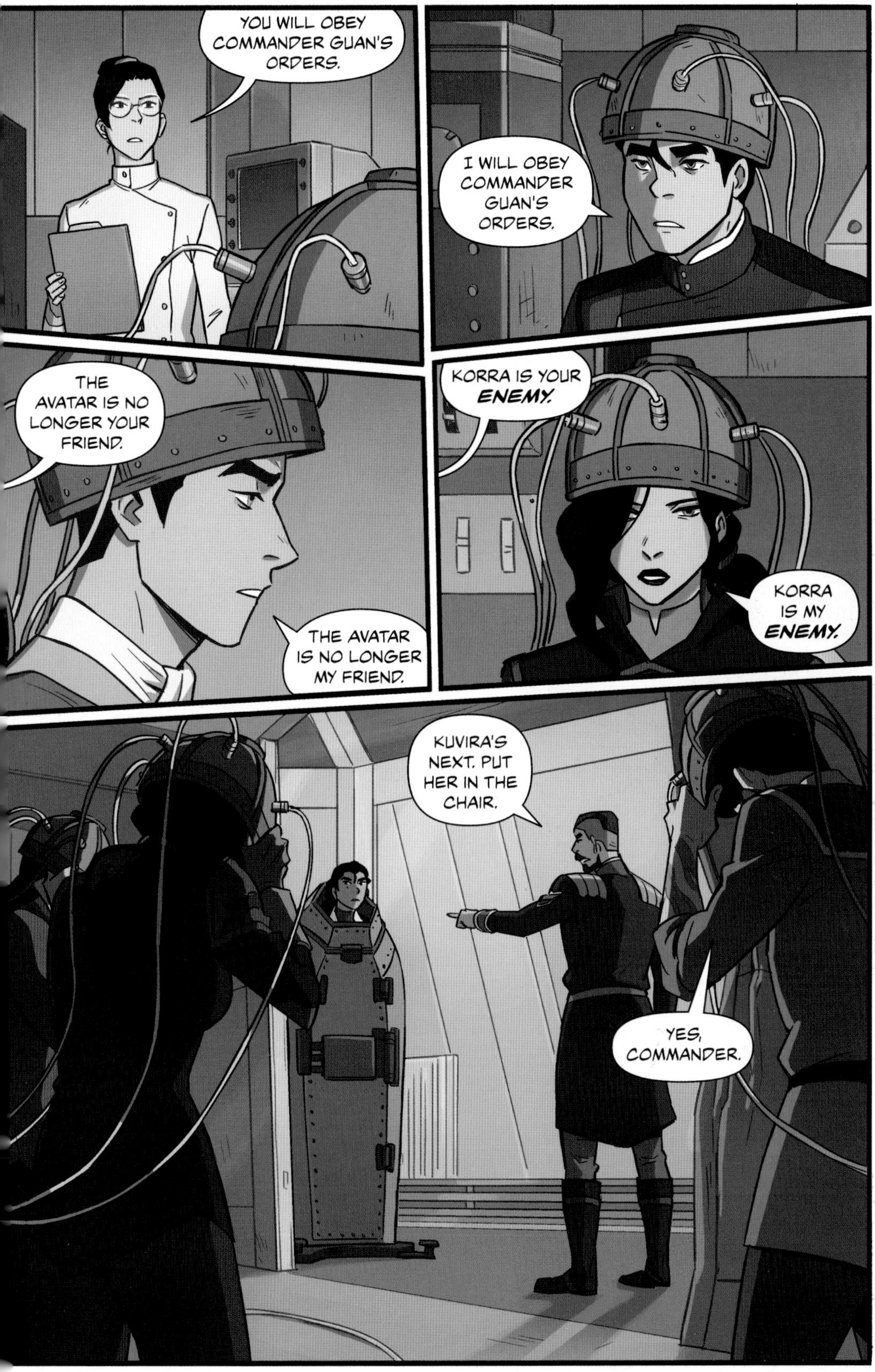
YOU WILL OBEY COMMANDER GUAN'S ORDERS.
I WILL OBEY COMMANDER GUAN'S ORDERS.
THE AVATAR IS NO LONGER YOUR FRIEND.
THE AVATAR IS NO LONGER MY FRIEND.
KORRA IS YOUR *ENEMY.*
KORRA IS MY *ENEMY.*
KUVIRA'S NEXT. PUT HER IN THE CHAIR.
YES, COMMANDER.

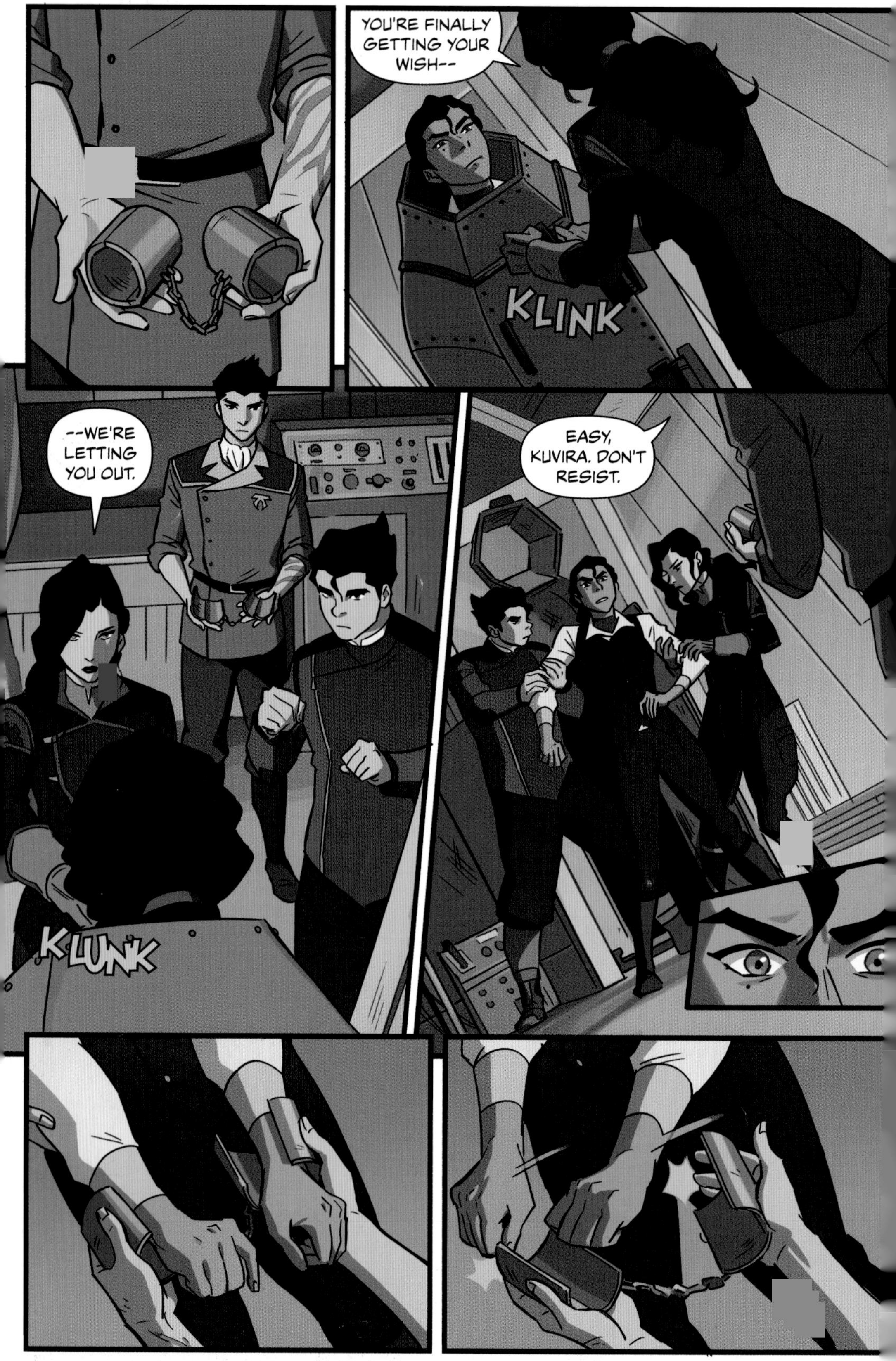
YOU'RE FINALLY GETTING YOUR WISH--
KLINK
--WE'RE LETTING YOU OUT.
KLUNK
EASY, KUVIRA. DON'T RESIST.

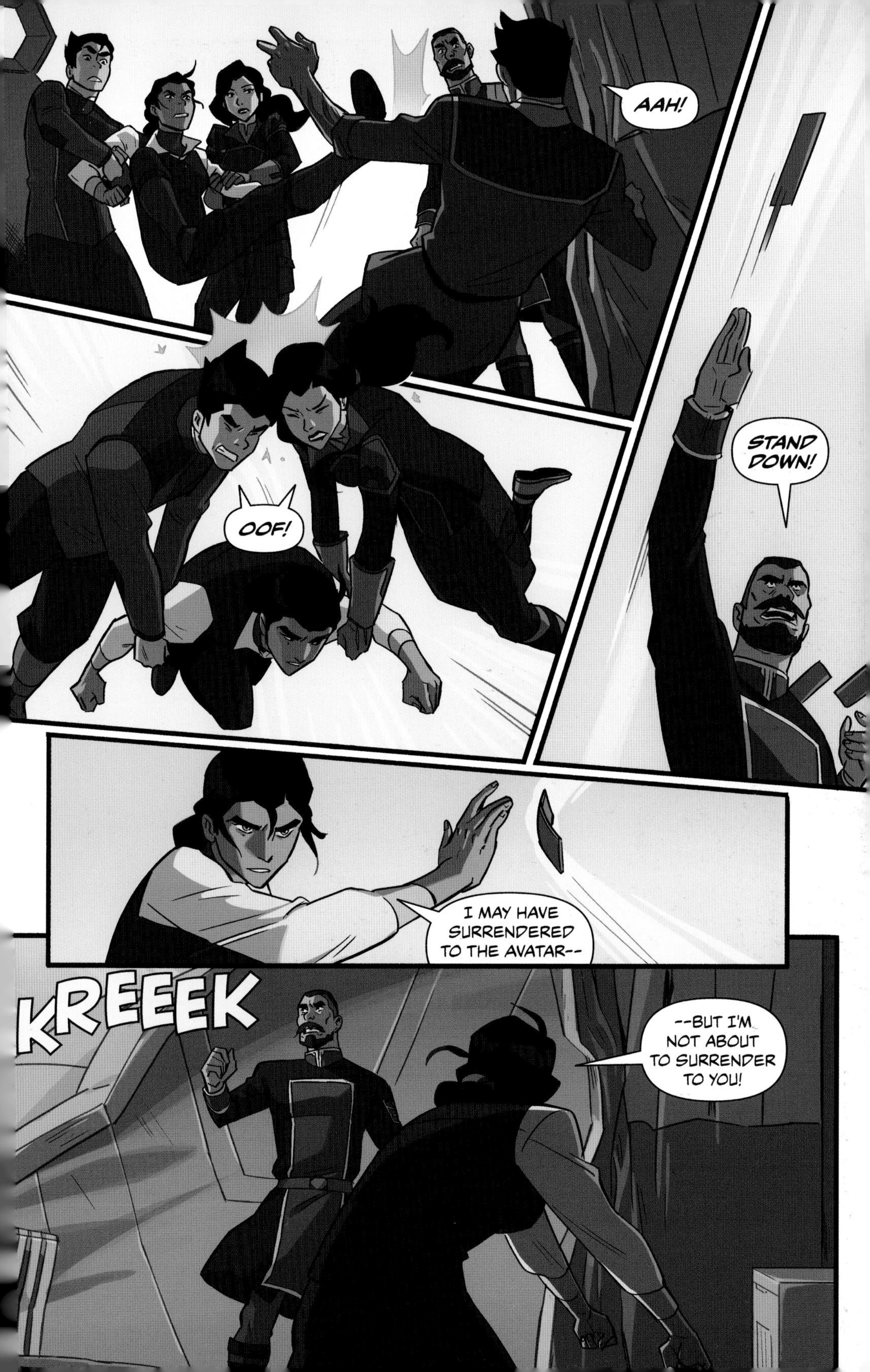
AAH!
OOF!
STAND DOWN!
I MAY HAVE SURRENDERED TO THE AVATAR--
KREEEK
--BUT I'M NOT ABOUT TO SURRENDER TO YOU!

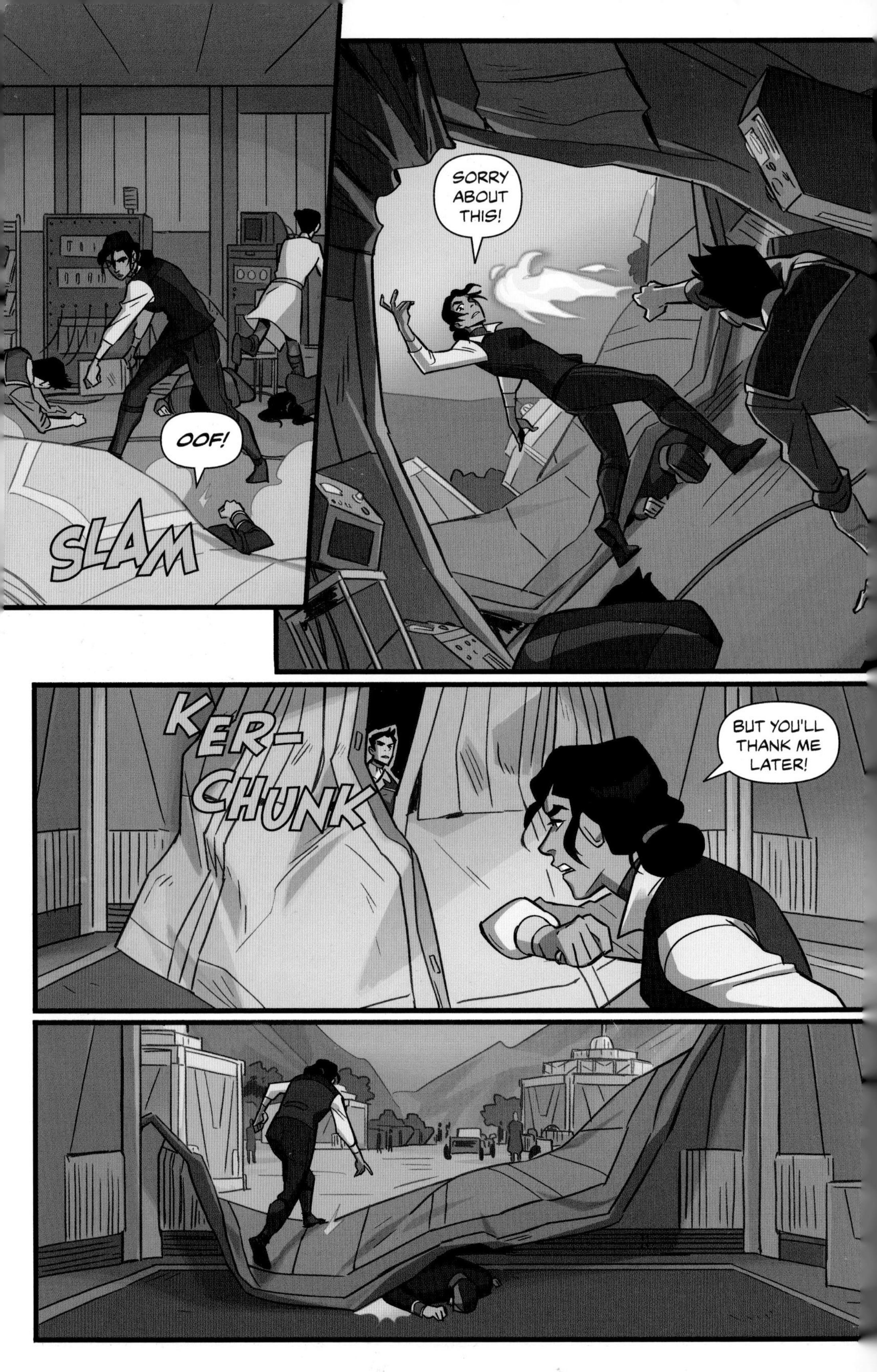
OOF!
SLAM
SORRY ABOUT THIS!
KER-CHUNK
BUT YOU'LL THANK ME LATER!

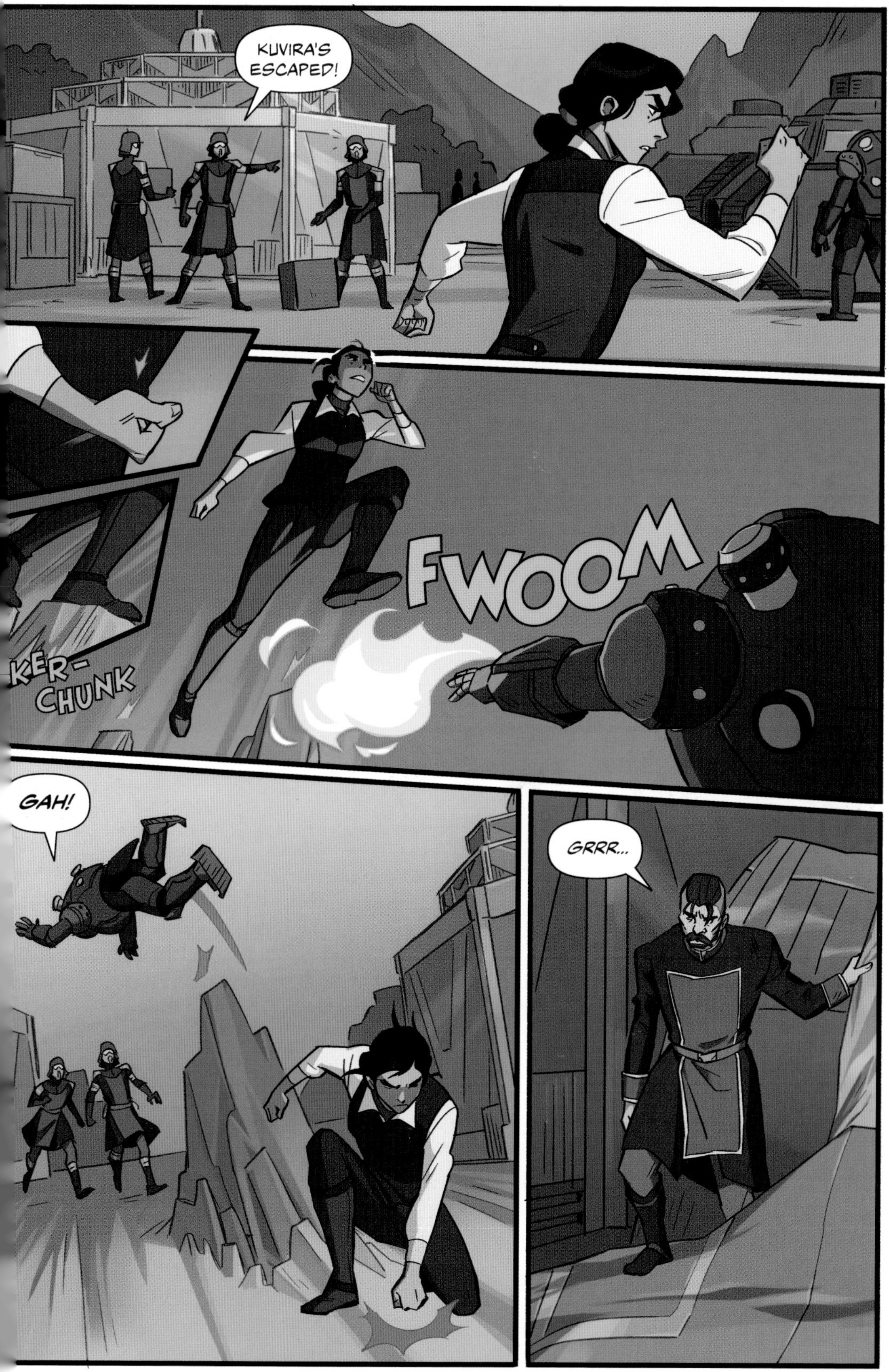
KUVIRA'S ESCAPED!
FWOOM
KER-CHUNK
GAH!
GRRR...

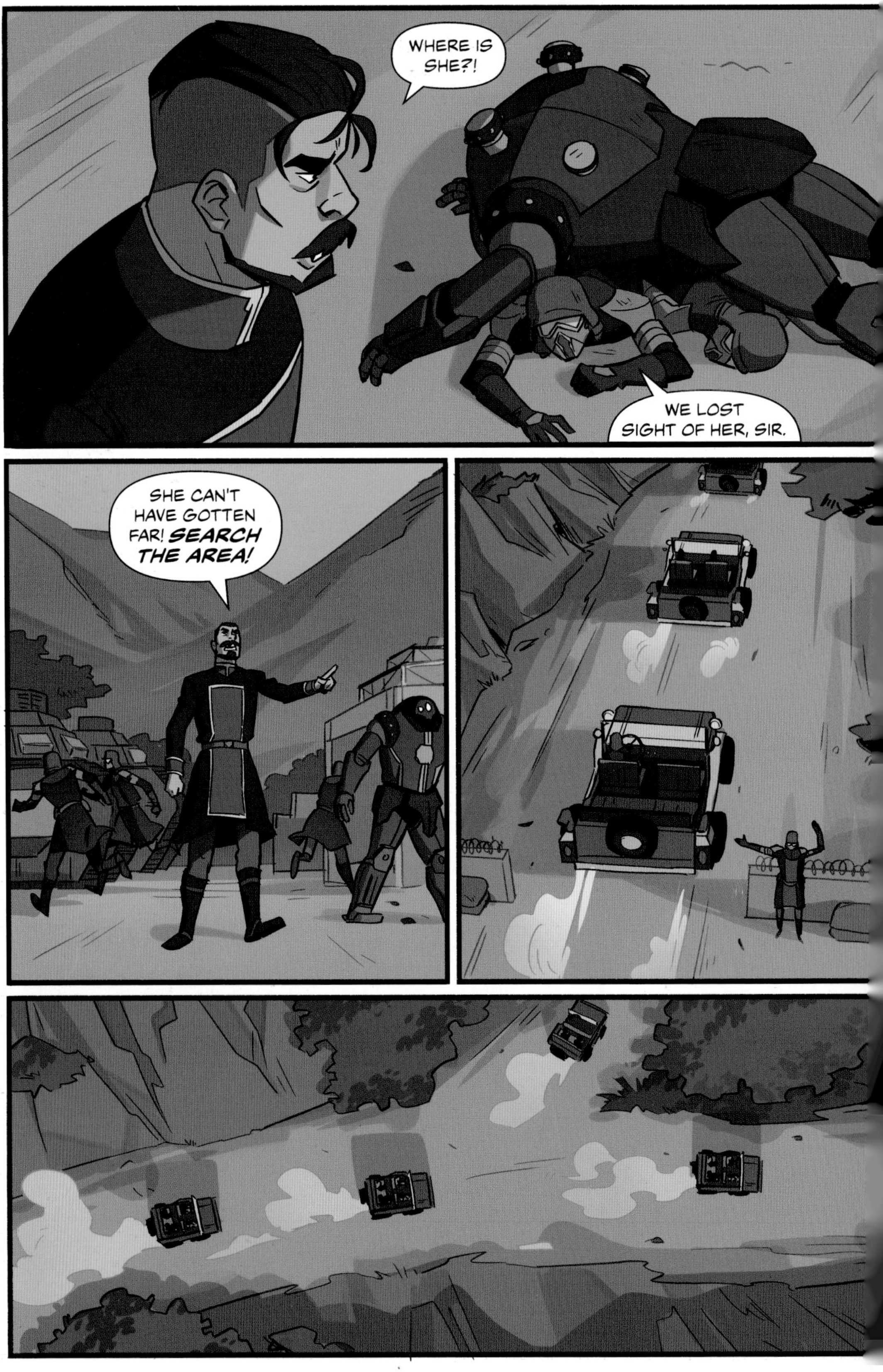
WHERE IS SHE?!
WE LOST SIGHT OF HER, SIR.
SHE CAN'T HAVE GOTTEN FAR! ***SEARCH THE AREA!***

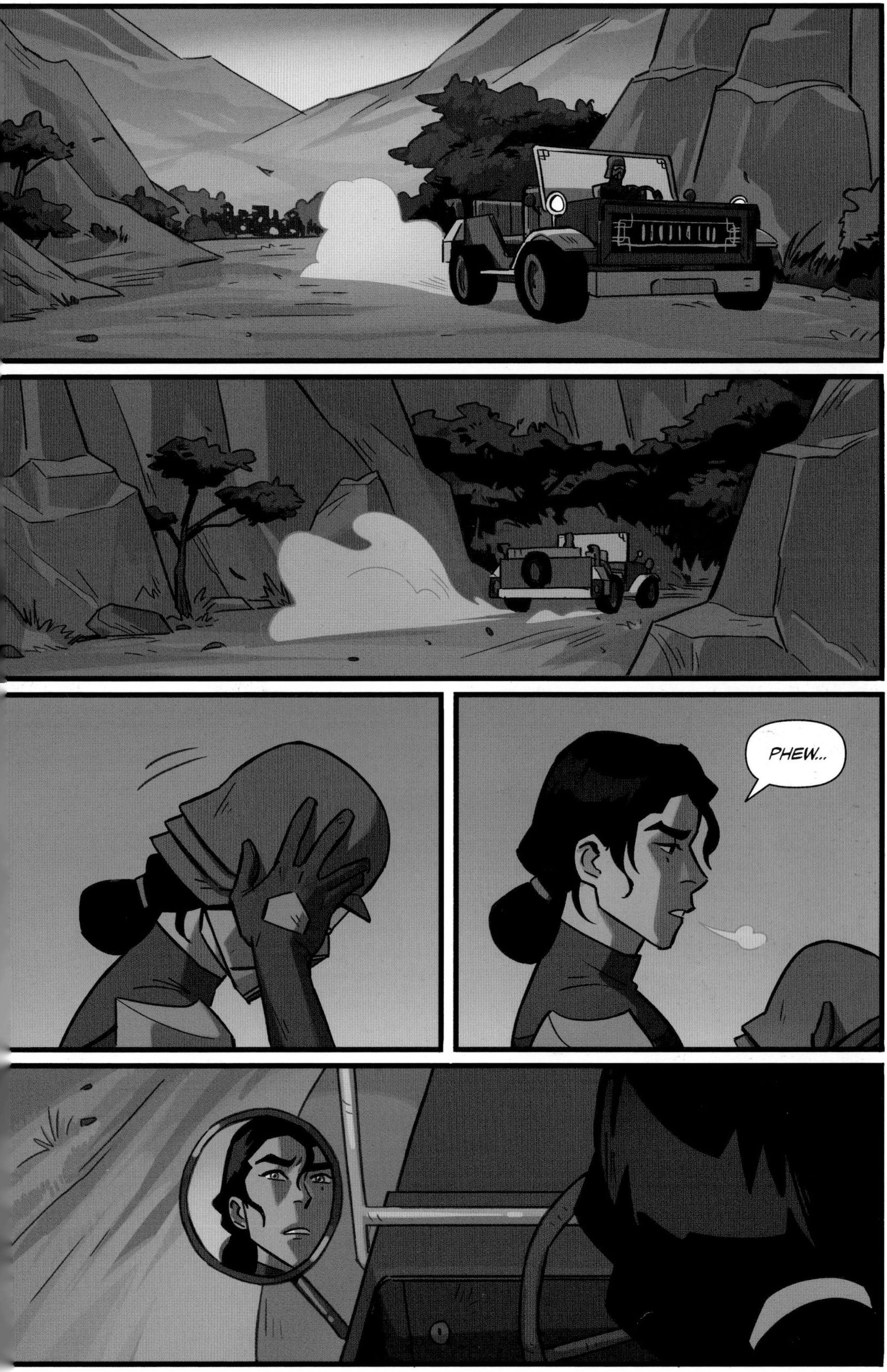
PHEW...

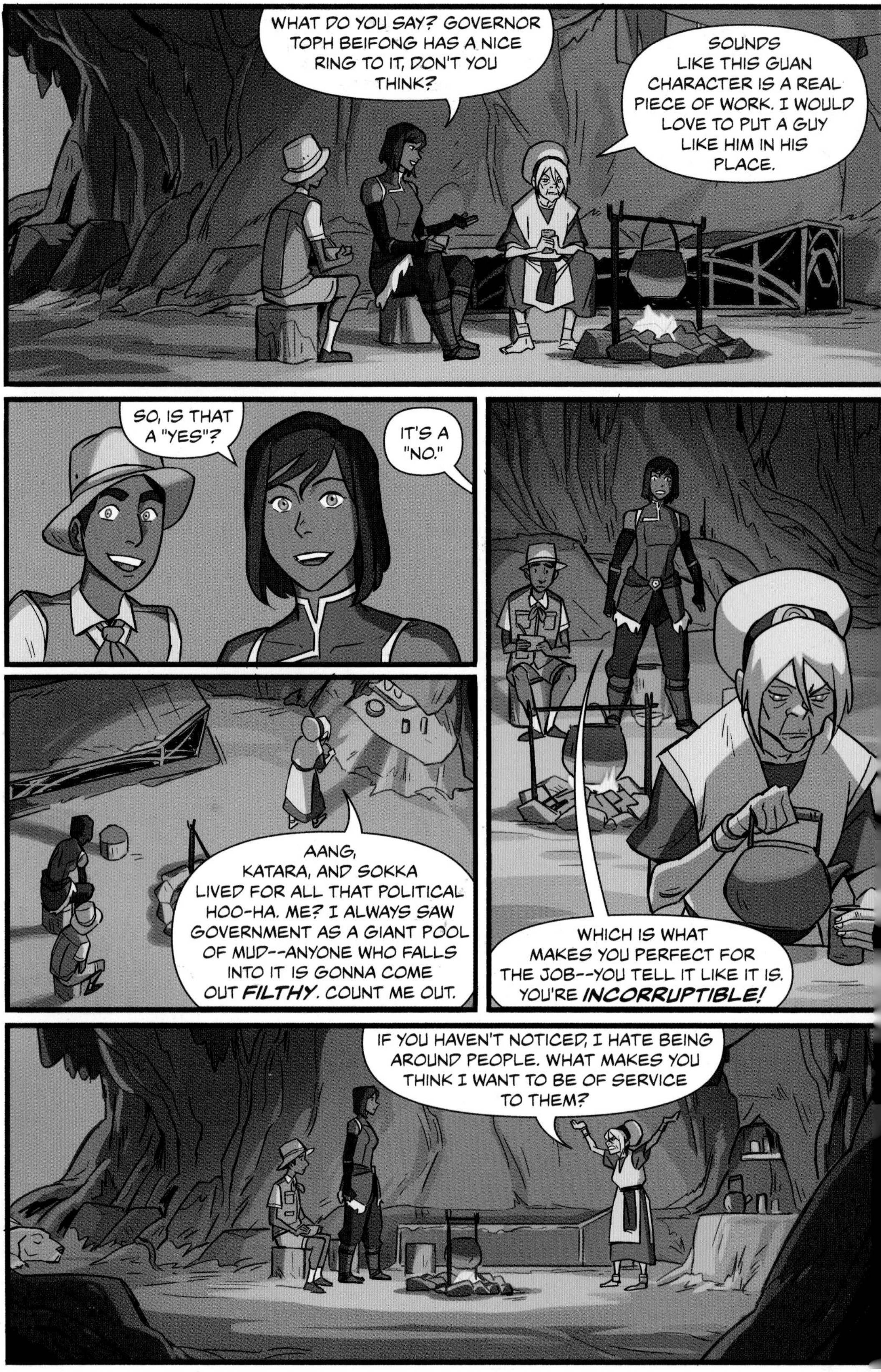
WHAT DO YOU SAY? GOVERNOR TOPH BEIFONG HAS A NICE RING TO IT, DON'T YOU THINK?
SOUNDS LIKE THIS GUAN CHARACTER IS A REAL PIECE OF WORK. I WOULD LOVE TO PUT A GUY LIKE HIM IN HIS PLACE.
SO, IS THAT A "YES"?
IT'S A "NO."
AANG, KATARA, AND SOKKA LIVED FOR ALL THAT POLITICAL HOO-HA. ME? I ALWAYS SAW GOVERNMENT AS A GIANT POOL OF MUD--ANYONE WHO FALLS INTO IT IS GONNA COME OUT FILTHY. COUNT ME OUT.
WHICH IS WHAT MAKES YOU PERFECT FOR THE JOB--YOU TELL IT LIKE IT IS. YOU'RE INCORRUPTIBLE!
IF YOU HAVEN'T NOTICED, I HATE BEING AROUND PEOPLE. WHAT MAKES YOU THINK I WANT TO BE OF SERVICE TO THEM?

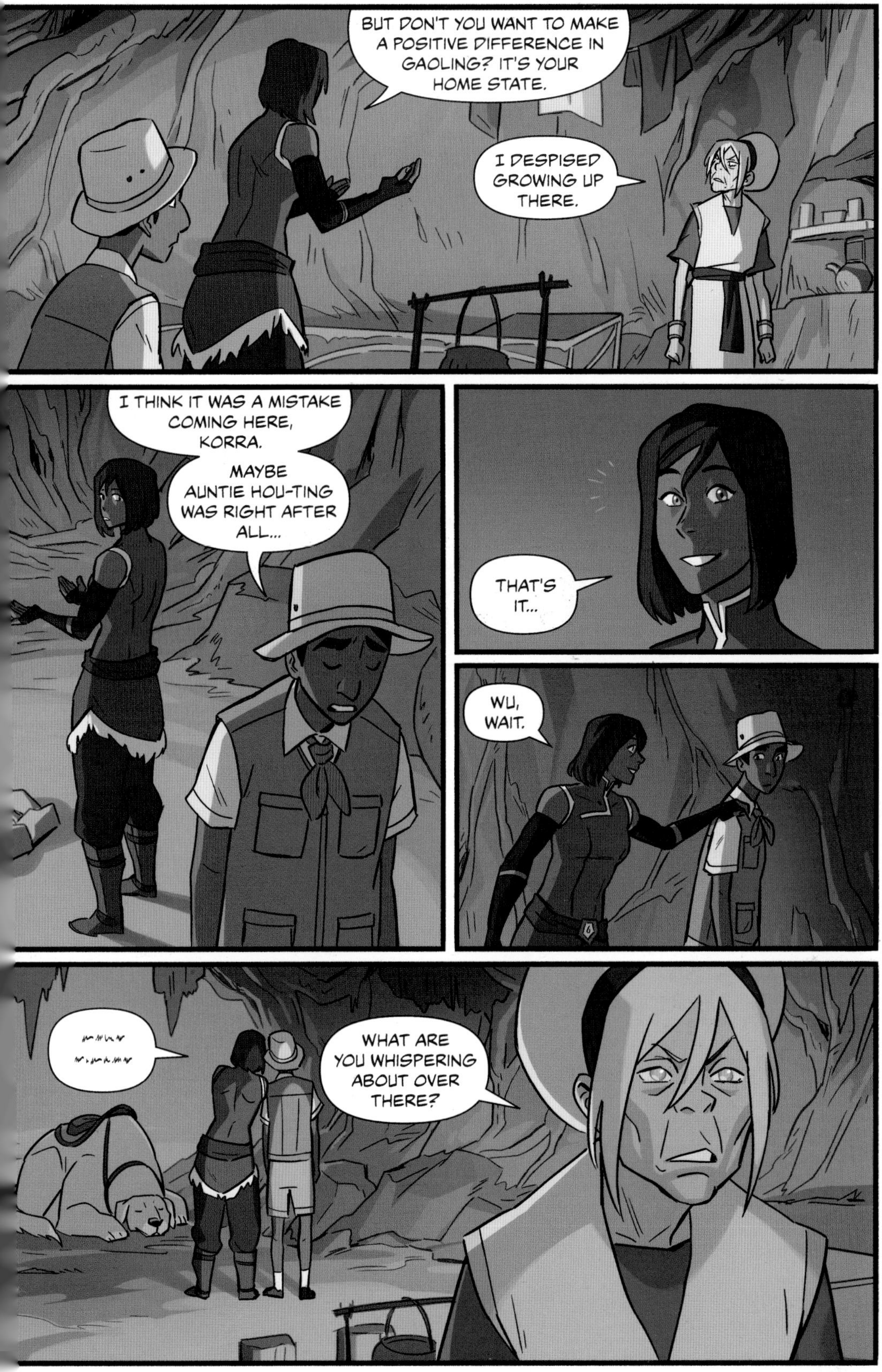
BUT DON'T YOU WANT TO MAKE A POSITIVE DIFFERENCE IN GAOLING? IT'S YOUR HOME STATE.
I DESPISED GROWING UP THERE.
I THINK IT WAS A MISTAKE COMING HERE, KORRA.
MAYBE AUNTIE HOU-TING WAS RIGHT AFTER ALL...
THAT'S IT...
WU, WAIT.
WHAT ARE YOU WHISPERING ABOUT OVER THERE?

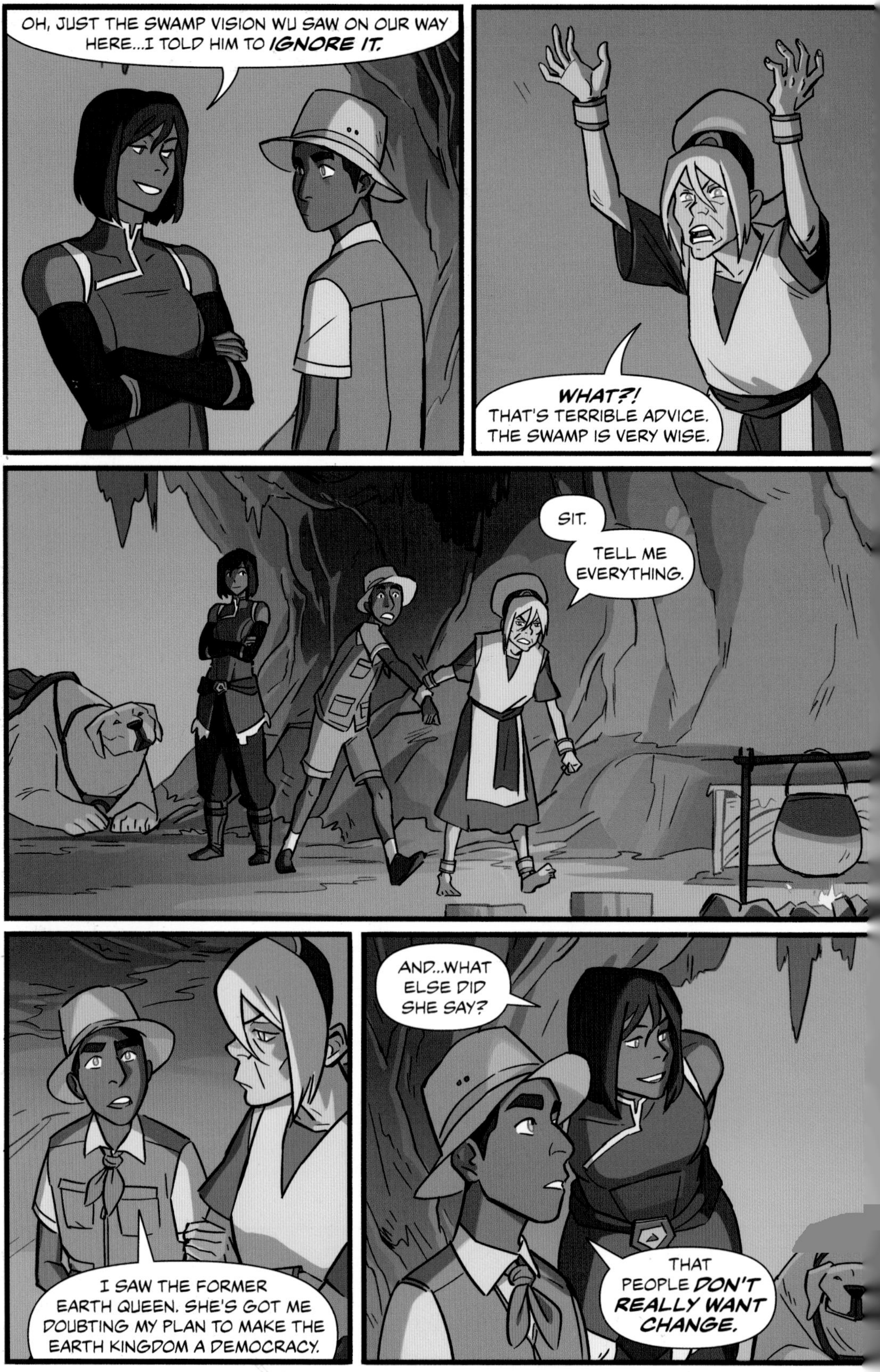
OH, JUST THE SWAMP VISION WU SAW ON OUR WAY HERE...I TOLD HIM TO IGNORE IT.
WHAT?! THAT'S TERRIBLE ADVICE. THE SWAMP IS VERY WISE.
SIT.
TELL ME EVERYTHING.
I SAW THE FORMER EARTH QUEEN. SHE'S GOT ME DOUBTING MY PLAN TO MAKE THE EARTH KINGDOM A DEMOCRACY.
AND...WHAT ELSE DID SHE SAY?
THAT PEOPLE DON'T REALLY WANT CHANGE.

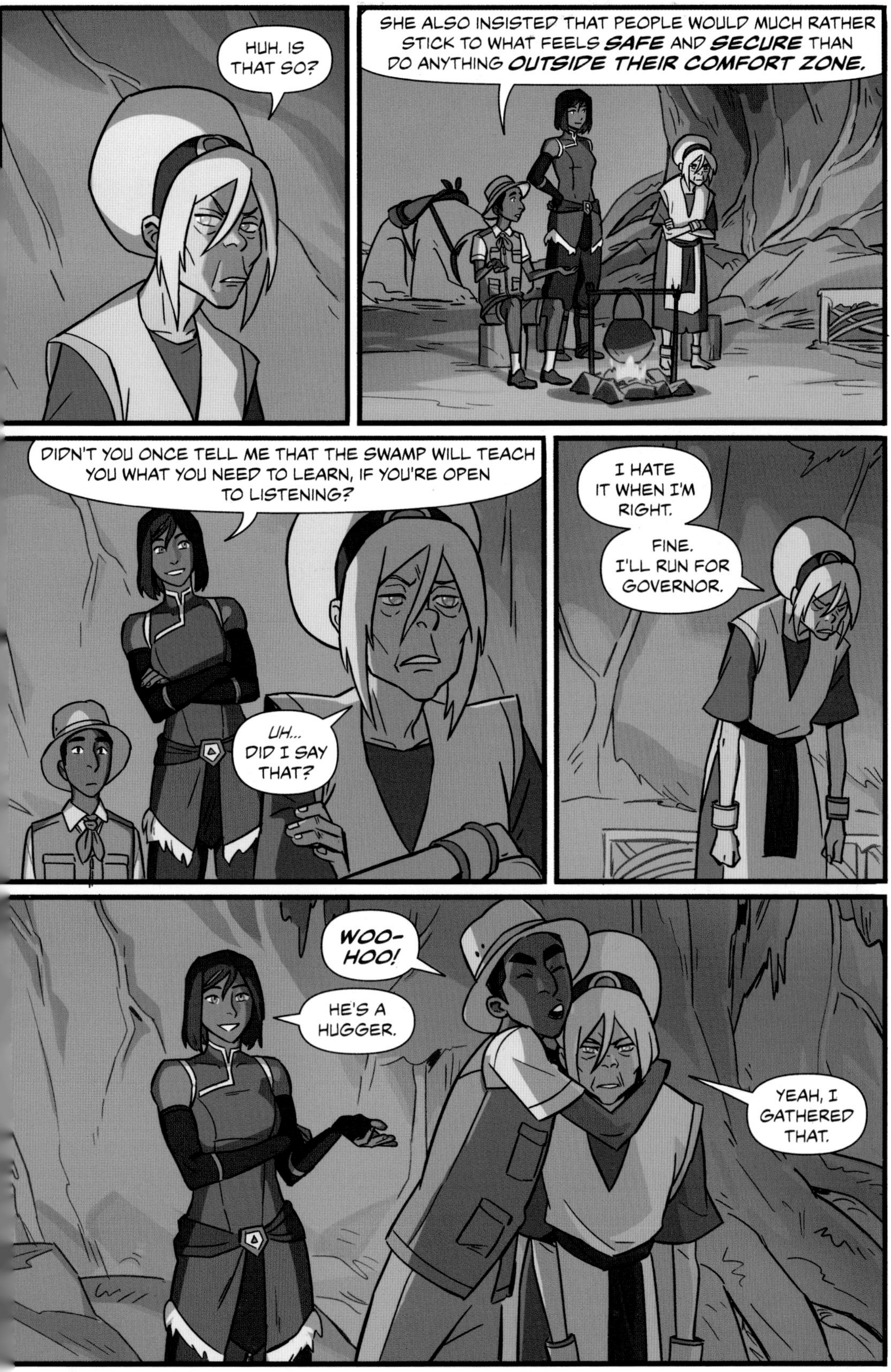
HUH. IS THAT SO?
SHE ALSO INSISTED THAT PEOPLE WOULD MUCH RATHER STICK TO WHAT FEELS SAFE AND SECURE THAN DO ANYTHING OUTSIDE THEIR COMFORT ZONE.
DIDN'T YOU ONCE TELL ME THAT THE SWAMP WILL TEACH YOU WHAT YOU NEED TO LEARN, IF YOU'RE OPEN TO LISTENING?
UH... DID I SAY THAT?
I HATE IT WHEN I'M RIGHT.
FINE. I'LL RUN FOR GOVERNOR.
WOO-HOO!
HE'S A HUGGER.
YEAH, I GATHERED THAT.

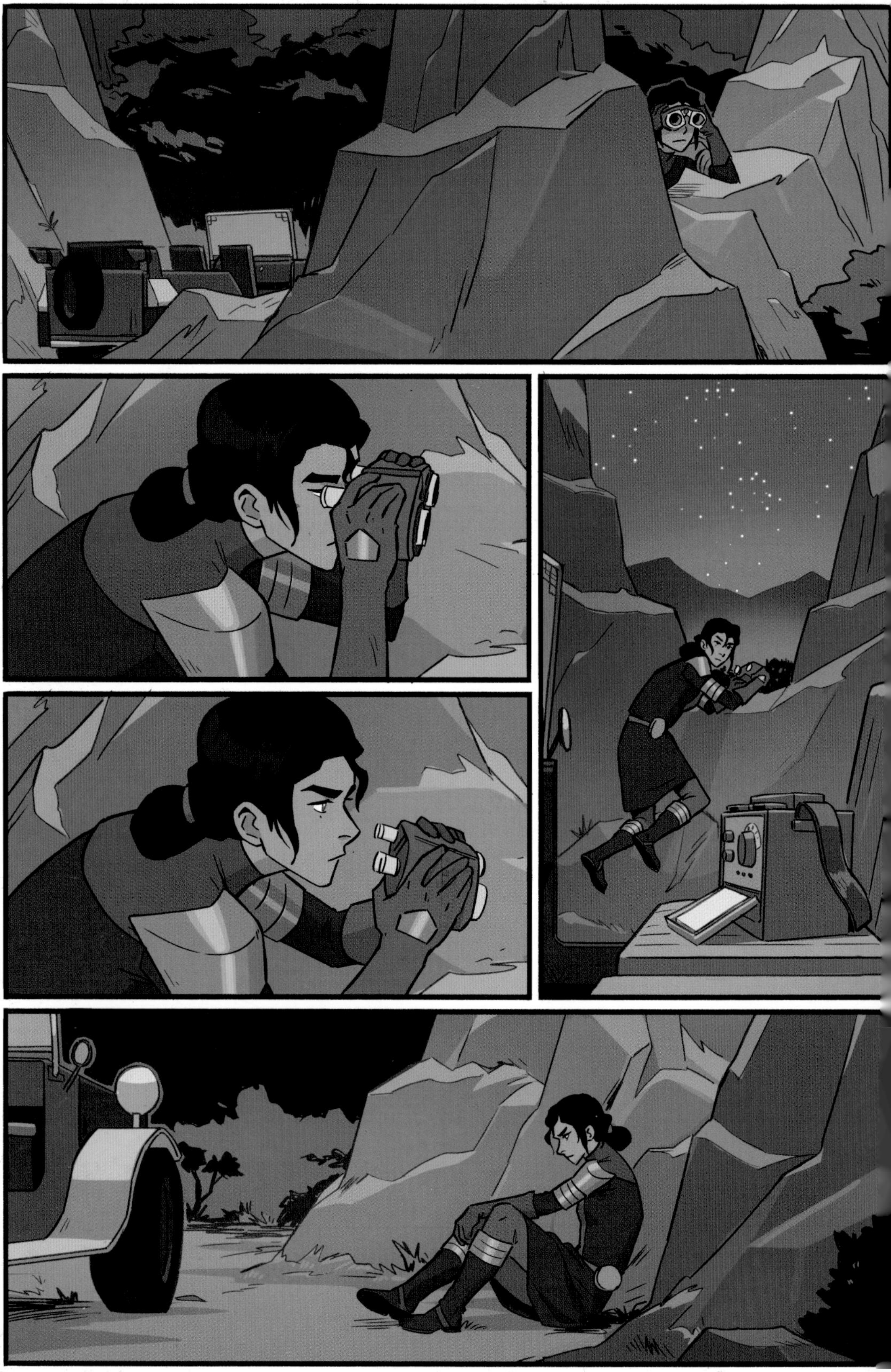

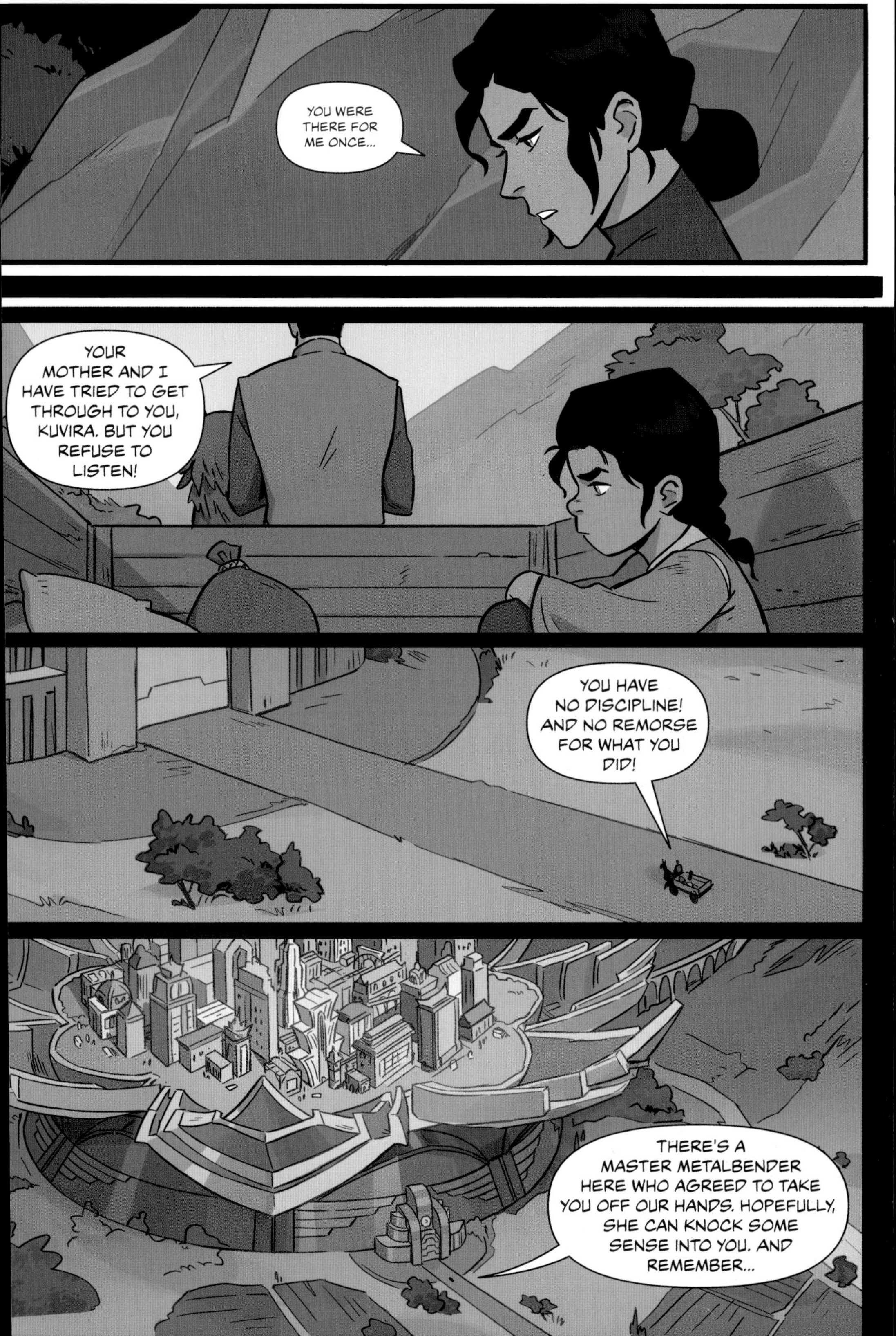
YOU WERE THERE FOR ME ONCE...
YOUR MOTHER AND I HAVE TRIED TO GET THROUGH TO YOU, KUVIRA. BUT YOU REFUSE TO LISTEN!
YOU HAVE NO DISCIPLINE! AND NO REMORSE FOR WHAT YOU DID!
THERE'S A MASTER METALBENDER HERE WHO AGREED TO TAKE YOU OFF OUR HANDS. HOPEFULLY, SHE CAN KNOCK SOME SENSE INTO YOU. AND REMEMBER...

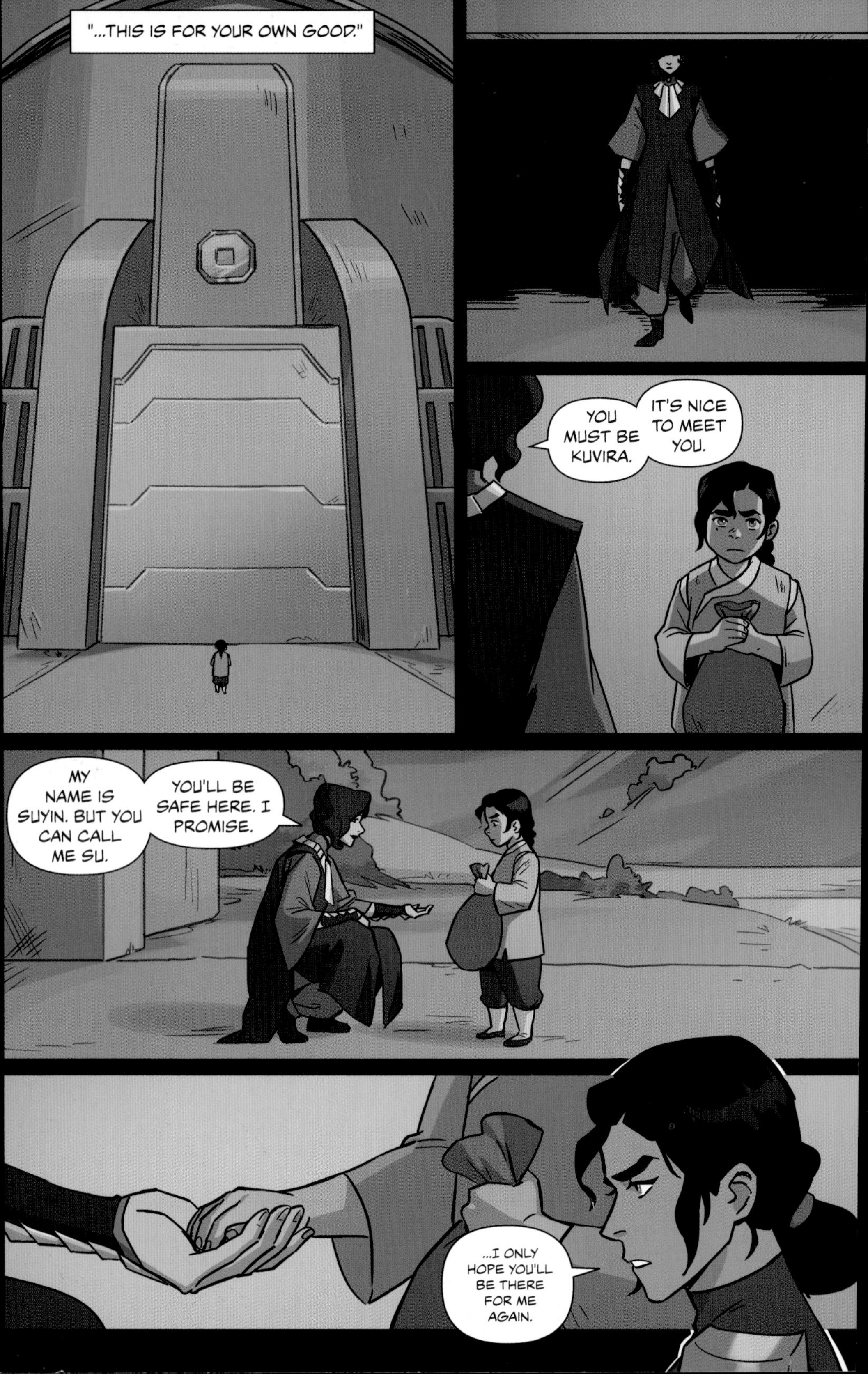
"...THIS IS FOR YOUR OWN GOOD."
YOU MUST BE KUVIRA.
IT'S NICE TO MEET YOU.
MY NAME IS SUYIN. BUT YOU CAN CALL ME SU.
YOU'LL BE SAFE HERE. I PROMISE.
...I ONLY HOPE YOU'LL BE THERE FOR ME AGAIN.

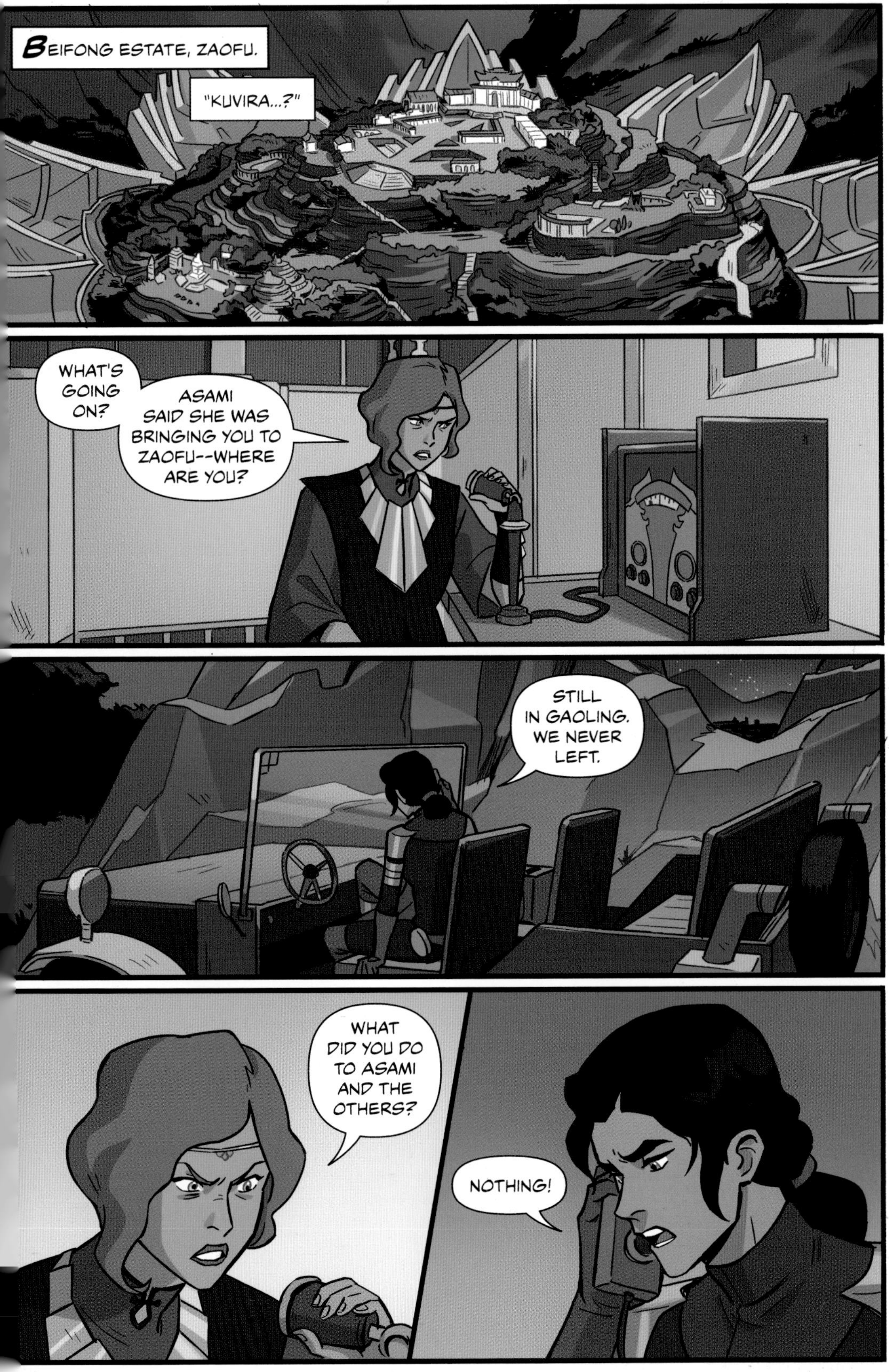
BEIFONG ESTATE, ZAOFU.
"KUVIRA...?"
WHAT'S GOING ON?
ASAMI SAID SHE WAS BRINGING YOU TO ZAOFU--WHERE ARE YOU?
STILL IN GAOLING. WE NEVER LEFT.
WHAT DID YOU DO TO ASAMI AND THE OTHERS?
NOTHING!

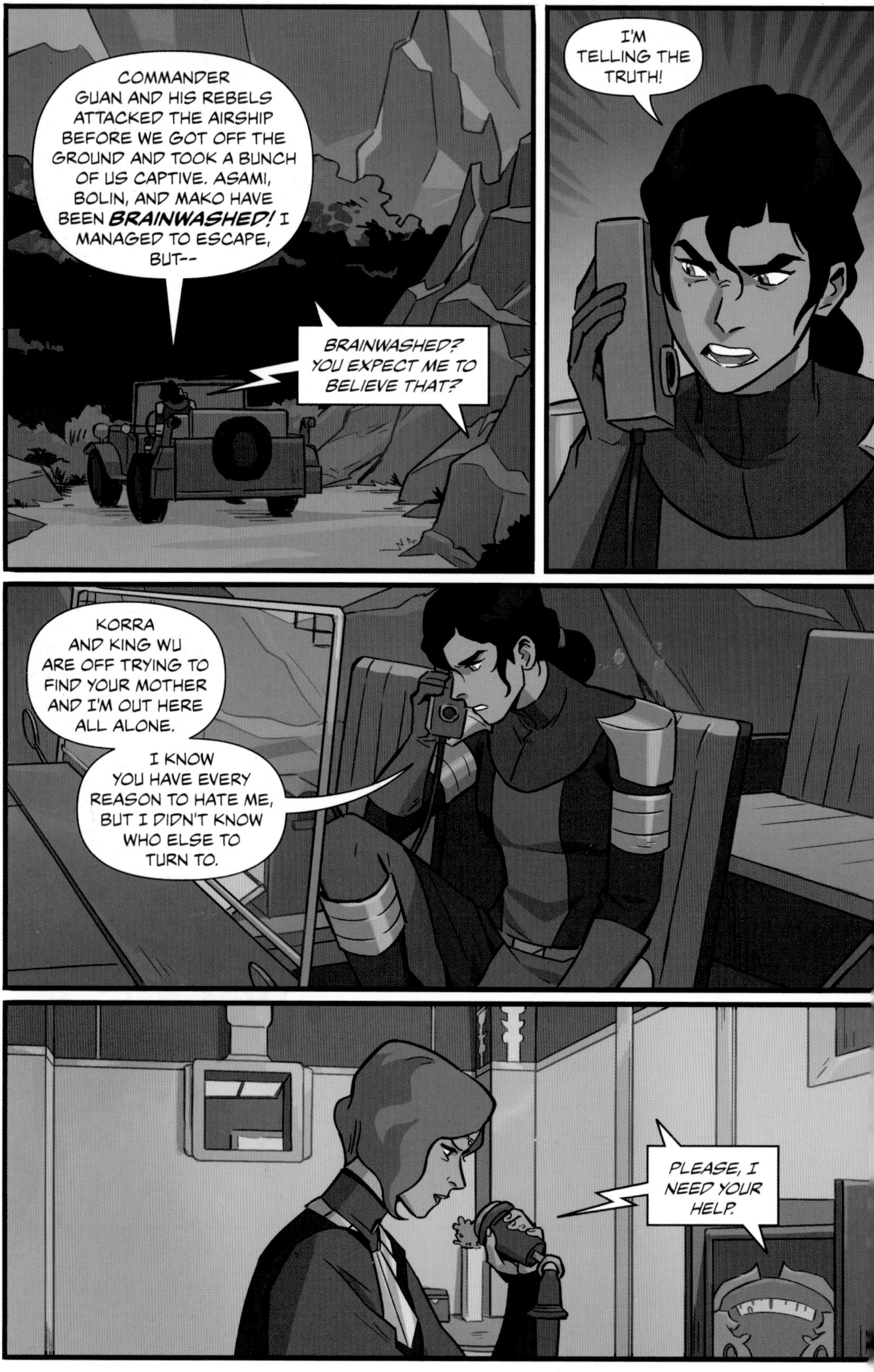
COMMANDER GUAN AND HIS REBELS ATTACKED THE AIRSHIP BEFORE WE GOT OFF THE GROUND AND TOOK A BUNCH OF US CAPTIVE. ASAMI, BOLIN, AND MAKO HAVE BEEN BRAINWASHED! I MANAGED TO ESCAPE, BUT--
BRAINWASHED? YOU EXPECT ME TO BELIEVE THAT?
I'M TELLING THE TRUTH!
KORRA AND KING WU ARE OFF TRYING TO FIND YOUR MOTHER AND I'M OUT HERE ALL ALONE.
I KNOW YOU HAVE EVERY REASON TO HATE ME, BUT I DIDN'T KNOW WHO ELSE TO TURN TO.
PLEASE, I NEED YOUR HELP.

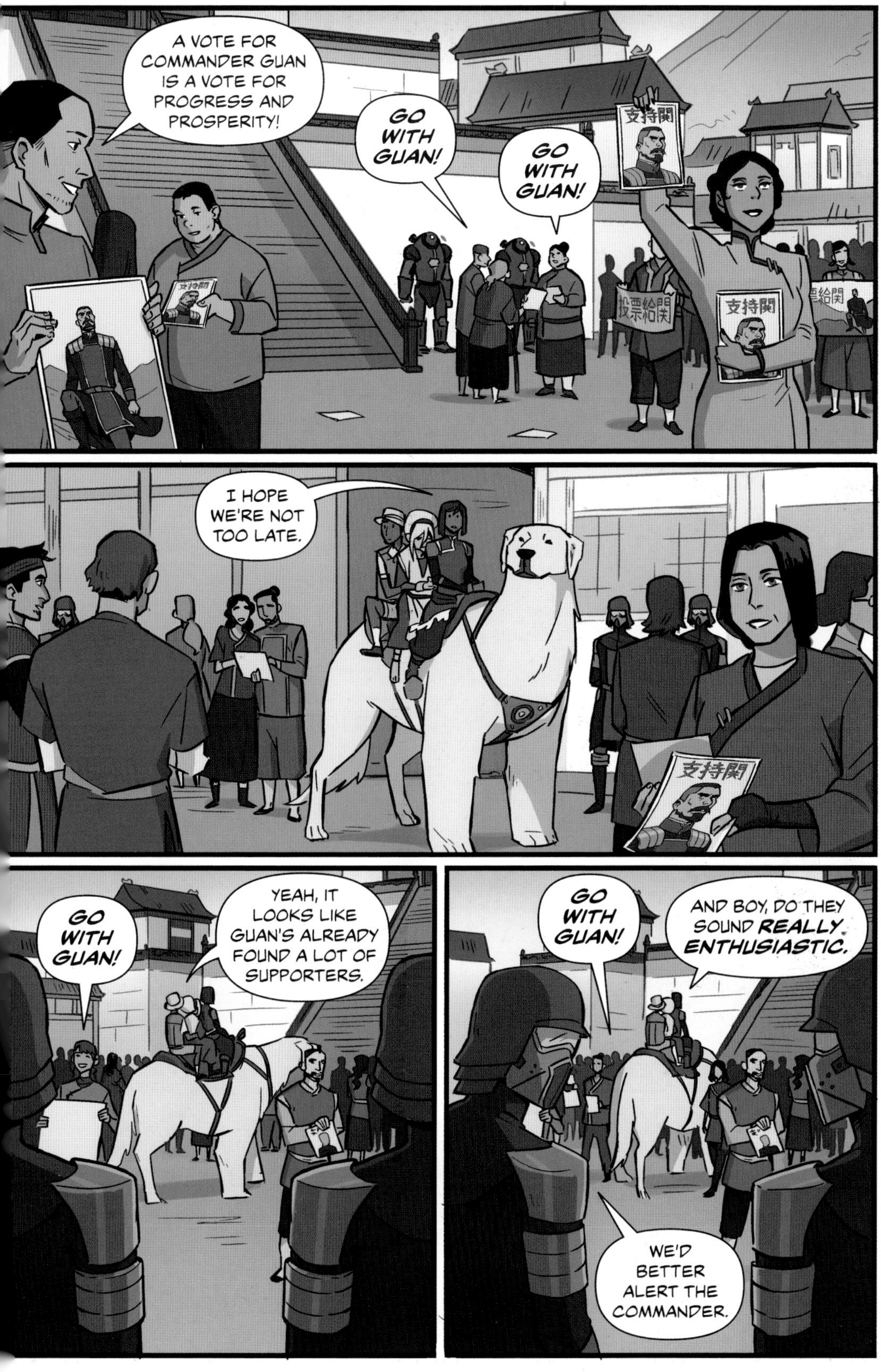
A VOTE FOR COMMANDER GUAN IS A VOTE FOR PROGRESS AND PROSPERITY!
GO WITH GUAN!
GO WITH GUAN!
支持関
投票給関
I HOPE WE'RE NOT TOO LATE.
支持関
GO WITH GUAN!
YEAH, IT LOOKS LIKE GUAN'S ALREADY FOUND A LOT OF SUPPORTERS.
GO WITH GUAN!
AND BOY, DO THEY SOUND **REALLY ENTHUSIASTIC.**
WE'D BETTER ALERT THE COMMANDER.

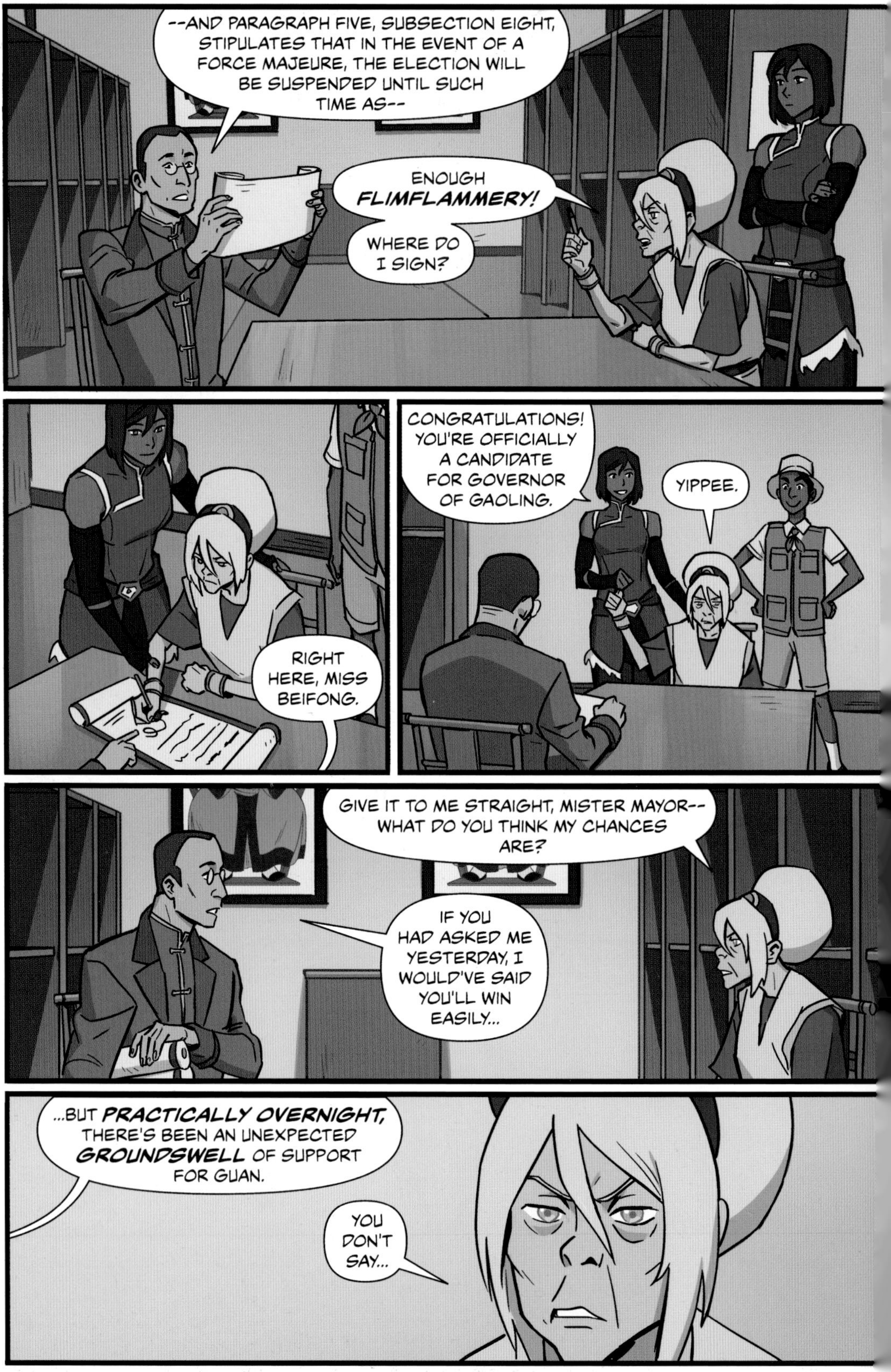
--AND PARAGRAPH FIVE, SUBSECTION EIGHT, STIPULATES THAT IN THE EVENT OF A FORCE MAJEURE, THE ELECTION WILL BE SUSPENDED UNTIL SUCH TIME AS--
ENOUGH FLIMFLAMMERY!
WHERE DO I SIGN?
RIGHT HERE, MISS BEIFONG.
CONGRATULATIONS! YOU'RE OFFICIALLY A CANDIDATE FOR GOVERNOR OF GAOLING.
YIPPEE.
GIVE IT TO ME STRAIGHT, MISTER MAYOR--WHAT DO YOU THINK MY CHANCES ARE?
IF YOU HAD ASKED ME YESTERDAY, I WOULD'VE SAID YOU'LL WIN EASILY...
...BUT PRACTICALLY OVERNIGHT, THERE'S BEEN AN UNEXPECTED GROUNDSWELL OF SUPPORT FOR GUAN.
YOU DON'T SAY...

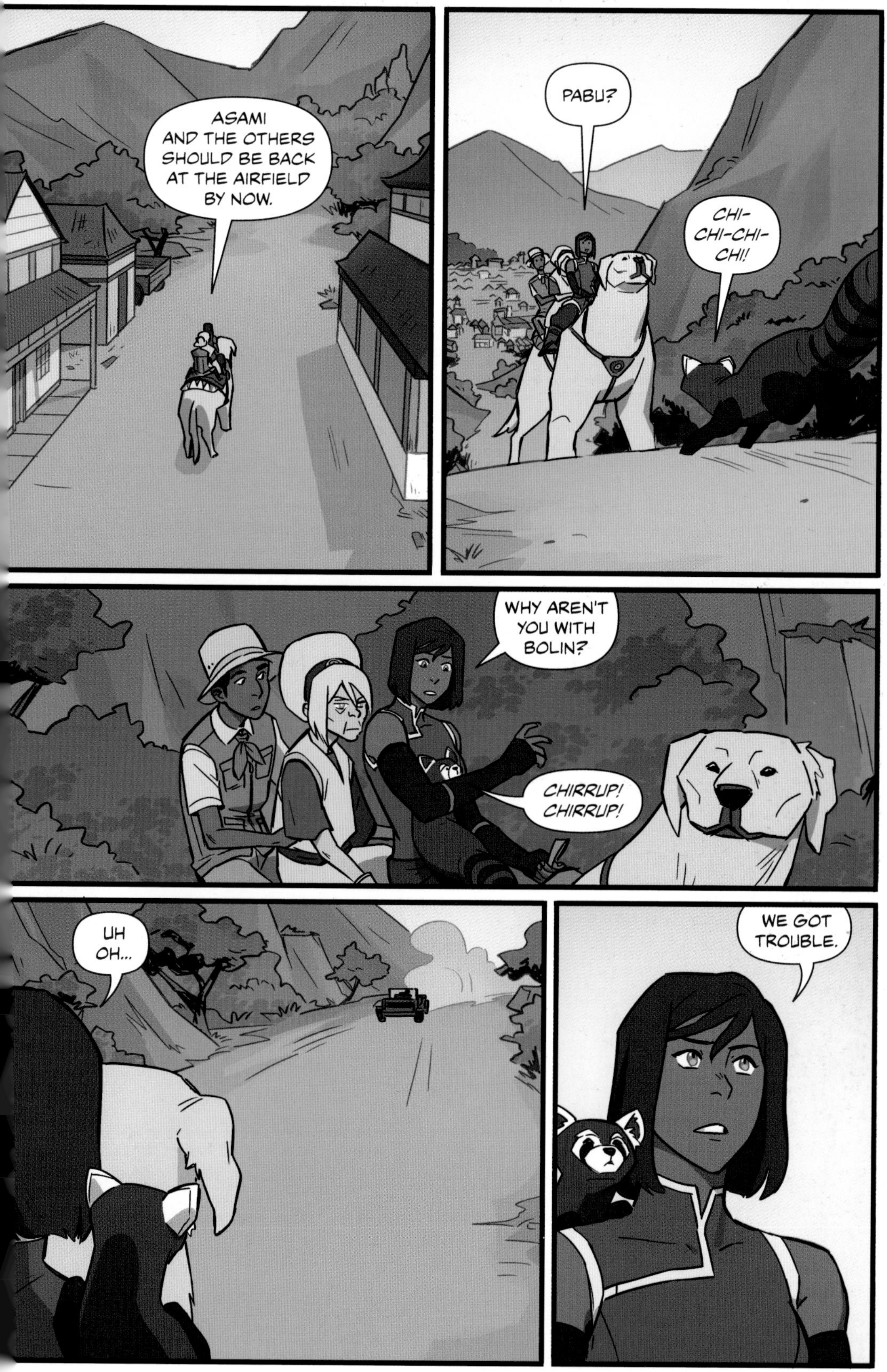
ASAMI AND THE OTHERS SHOULD BE BACK AT THE AIRFIELD BY NOW.
PABU?
CHI-CHI-CHI-CHI!
WHY AREN'T YOU WITH BOLIN?
CHIRRUP! CHIRRUP!
UH OH...
WE GOT TROUBLE.

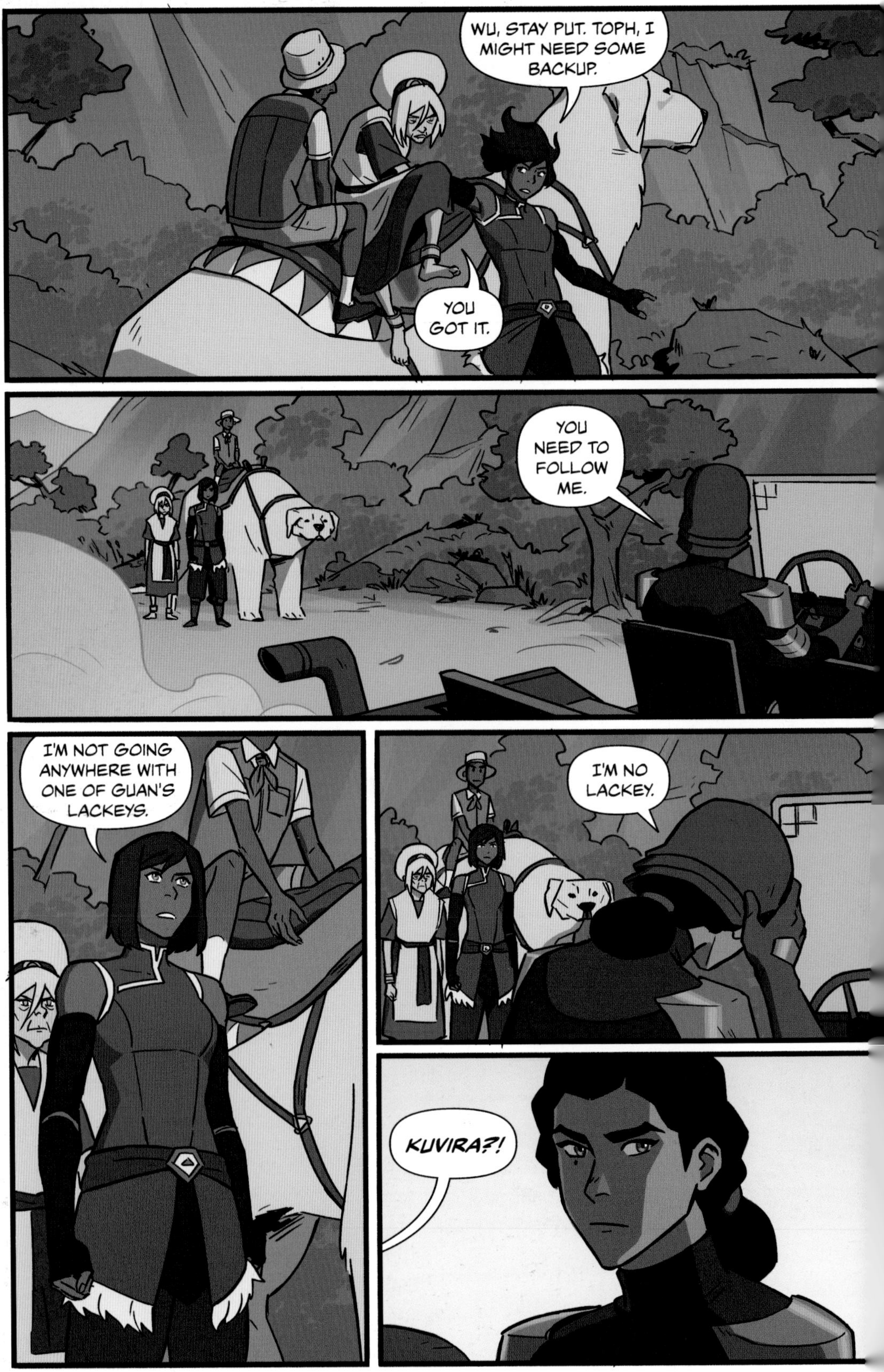
WU, STAY PUT. TOPH, I MIGHT NEED SOME BACKUP.
YOU GOT IT.
YOU NEED TO FOLLOW ME.
I'M NOT GOING ANYWHERE WITH ONE OF GUAN'S LACKEYS.
I'M NO LACKEY.
KUVIRA?!

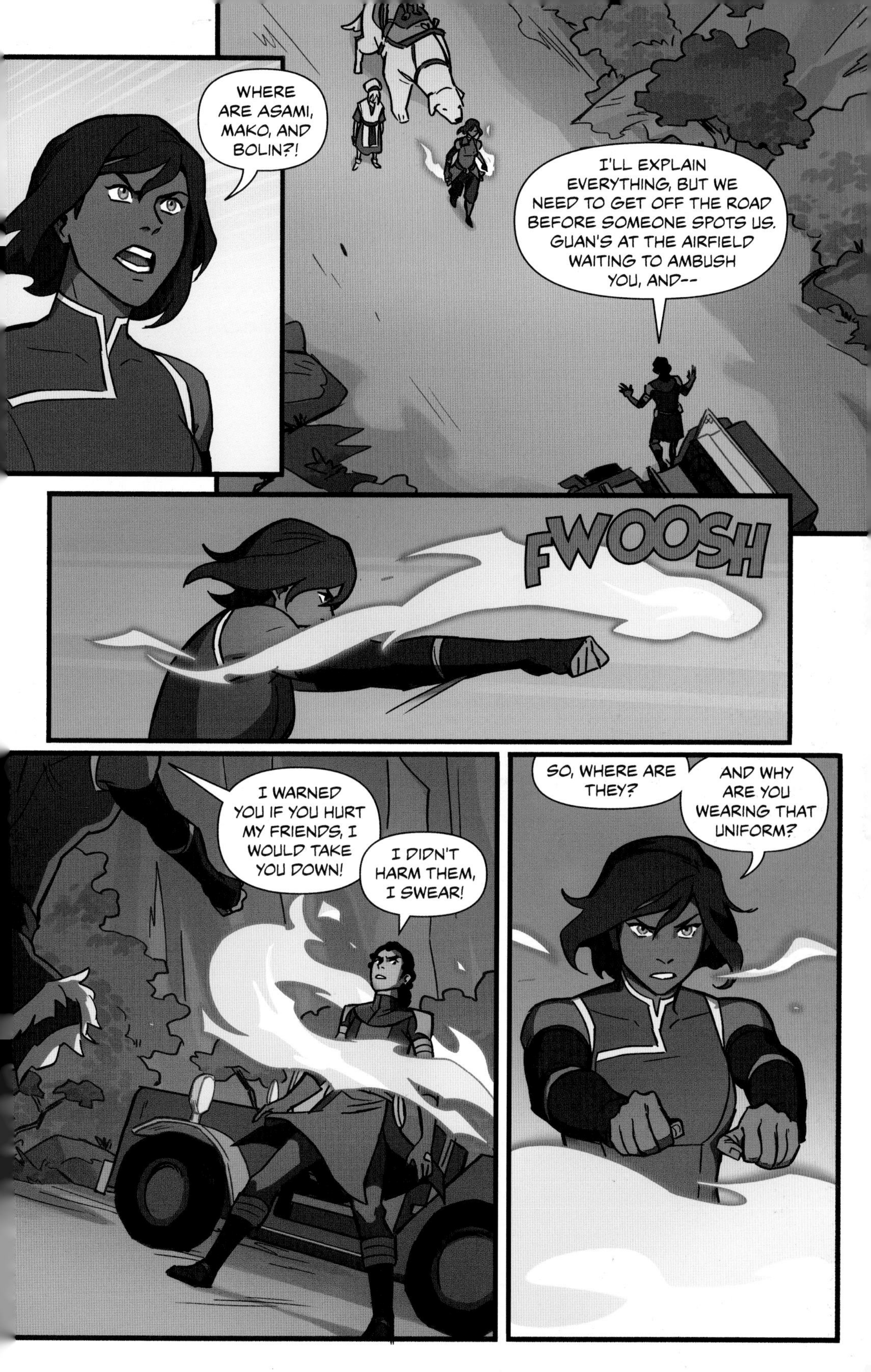
WHERE ARE ASAMI, MAKO, AND BOLIN?!
I'LL EXPLAIN EVERYTHING, BUT WE NEED TO GET OFF THE ROAD BEFORE SOMEONE SPOTS US. GUAN'S AT THE AIRFIELD WAITING TO AMBUSH YOU, AND--
FWOOSH
I WARNED YOU IF YOU HURT MY FRIENDS, I WOULD TAKE YOU DOWN!
I DIDN'T HARM THEM, I SWEAR!
SO, WHERE ARE THEY?
AND WHY ARE YOU WEARING THAT UNIFORM?

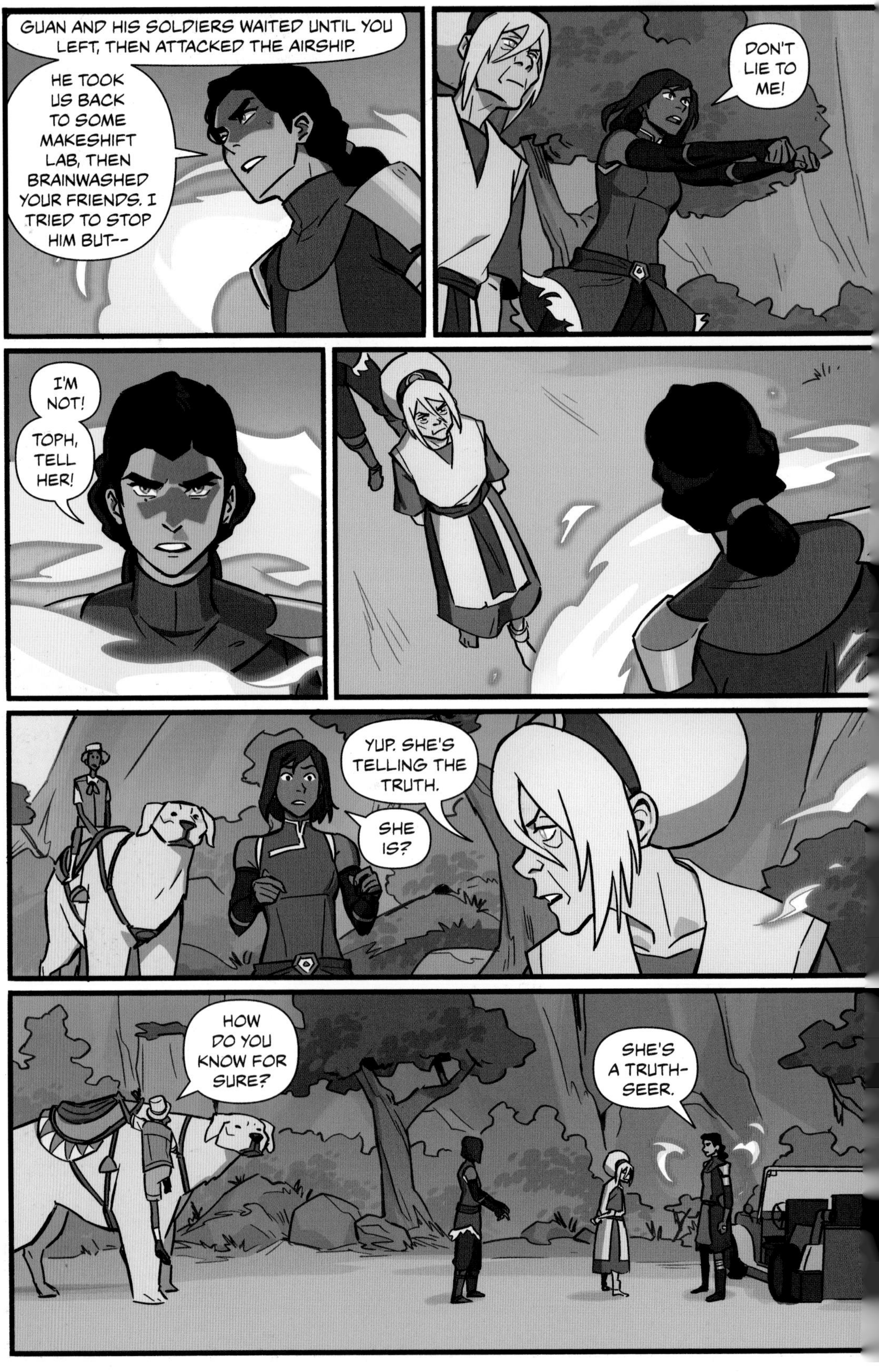
GUAN AND HIS SOLDIERS WAITED UNTIL YOU LEFT, THEN ATTACKED THE AIRSHIP.
HE TOOK US BACK TO SOME MAKESHIFT LAB, THEN BRAINWASHED YOUR FRIENDS. I TRIED TO STOP HIM BUT--
DON'T LIE TO ME!
I'M NOT!
TOPH, TELL HER!
YUP. SHE'S TELLING THE TRUTH.
SHE IS?
HOW DO YOU KNOW FOR SURE?
SHE'S A TRUTH-SEER.

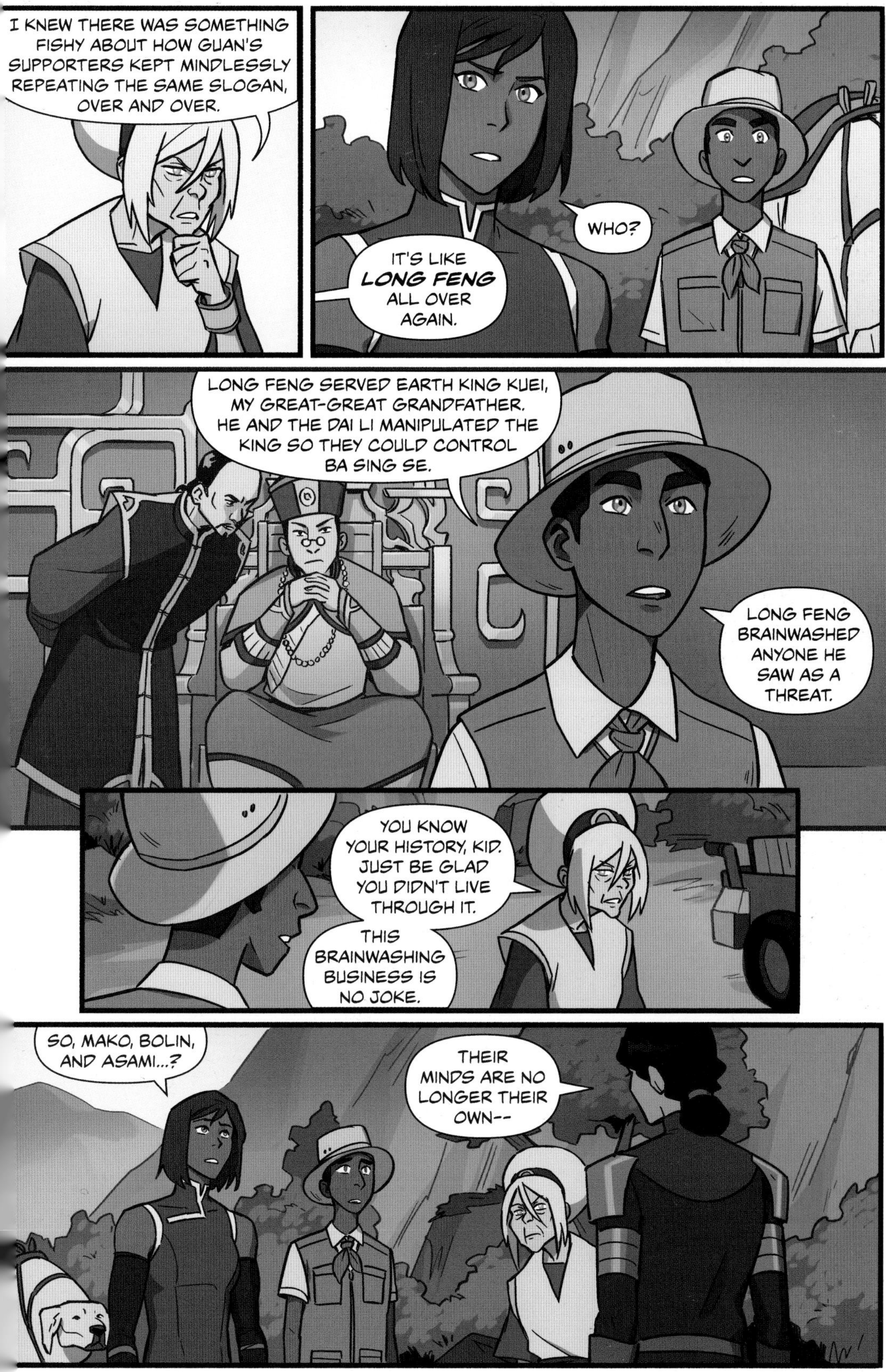
I KNEW THERE WAS SOMETHING FISHY ABOUT HOW GUAN'S SUPPORTERS KEPT MINDLESSLY REPEATING THE SAME SLOGAN, OVER AND OVER.
IT'S LIKE LONG FENG ALL OVER AGAIN.
WHO?
LONG FENG SERVED EARTH KING KUEI, MY GREAT-GREAT GRANDFATHER. HE AND THE DAI LI MANIPULATED THE KING SO THEY COULD CONTROL BA SING SE.
LONG FENG BRAINWASHED ANYONE HE SAW AS A THREAT.
YOU KNOW YOUR HISTORY, KID. JUST BE GLAD YOU DIDN'T LIVE THROUGH IT.
THIS BRAINWASHING BUSINESS IS NO JOKE.
SO, MAKO, BOLIN, AND ASAMI...?
THEIR MINDS ARE NO LONGER THEIR OWN--

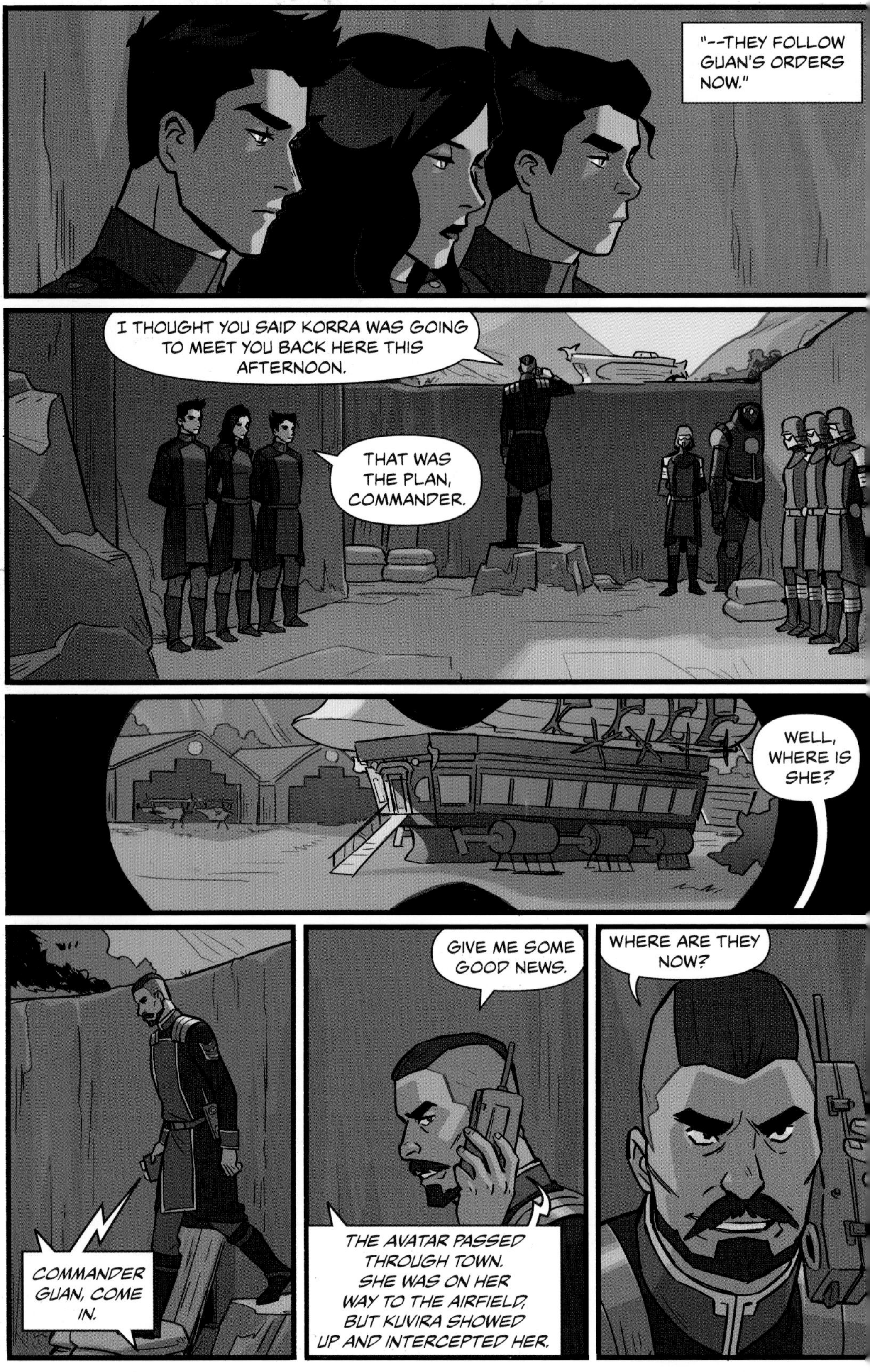
"--THEY FOLLOW GUAN'S ORDERS NOW."
I THOUGHT YOU SAID KORRA WAS GOING TO MEET YOU BACK HERE THIS AFTERNOON.
THAT WAS THE PLAN, COMMANDER.
WELL, WHERE IS SHE?
COMMANDER GUAN, COME IN.
GIVE ME SOME GOOD NEWS.
THE AVATAR PASSED THROUGH TOWN. SHE WAS ON HER WAY TO THE AIRFIELD, BUT KUVIRA SHOWED UP AND INTERCEPTED HER.
WHERE ARE THEY NOW?

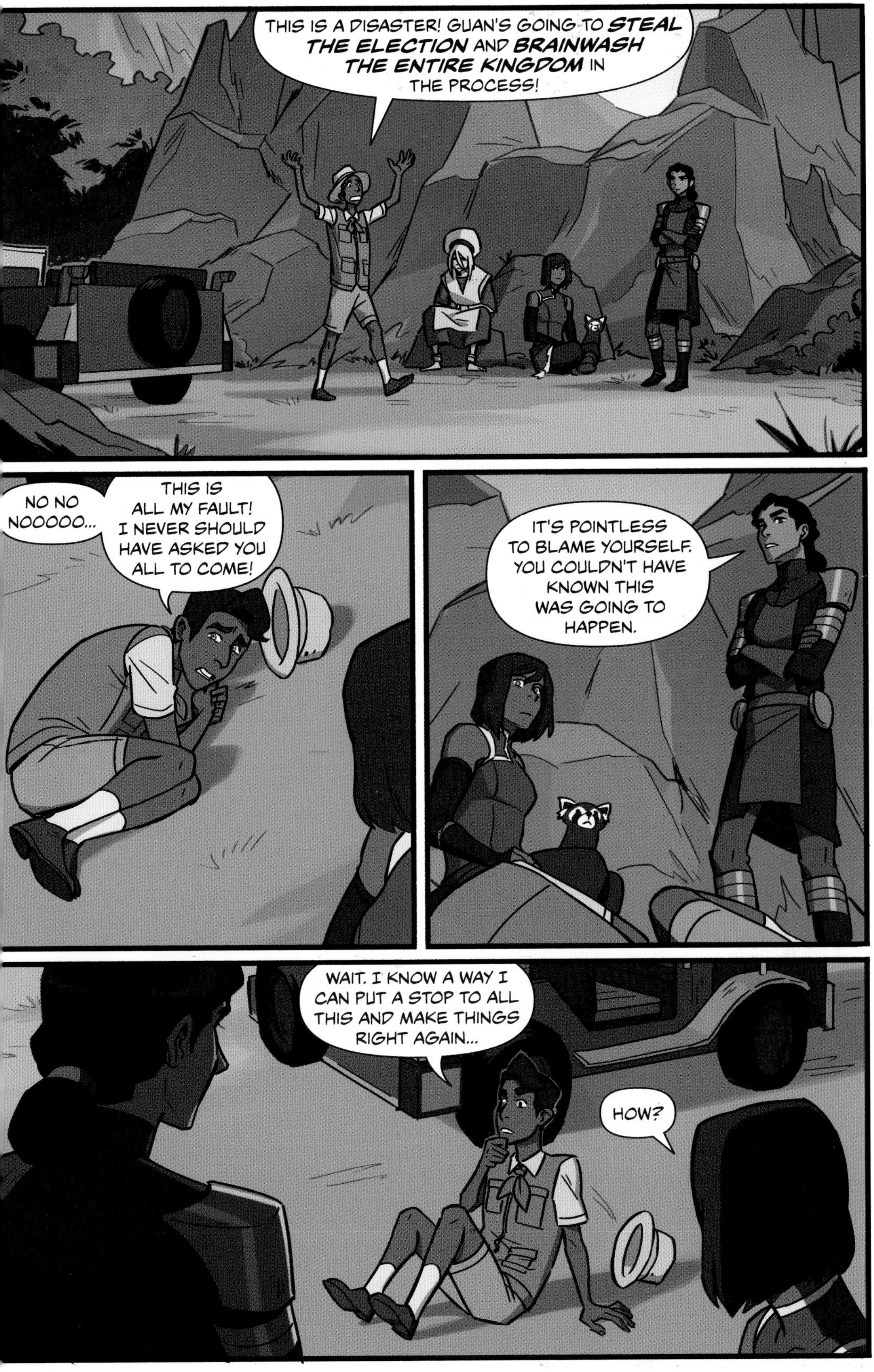
THIS IS A DISASTER! GUAN'S GOING TO **STEAL THE ELECTION** AND **BRAINWASH THE ENTIRE KINGDOM** IN THE PROCESS!
NO NO NOOOOO...
THIS IS ALL MY FAULT! I NEVER SHOULD HAVE ASKED YOU ALL TO COME!
IT'S POINTLESS TO BLAME YOURSELF. YOU COULDN'T HAVE KNOWN THIS WAS GOING TO HAPPEN.
WAIT. I KNOW A WAY I CAN PUT A STOP TO ALL THIS AND MAKE THINGS RIGHT AGAIN...
HOW?

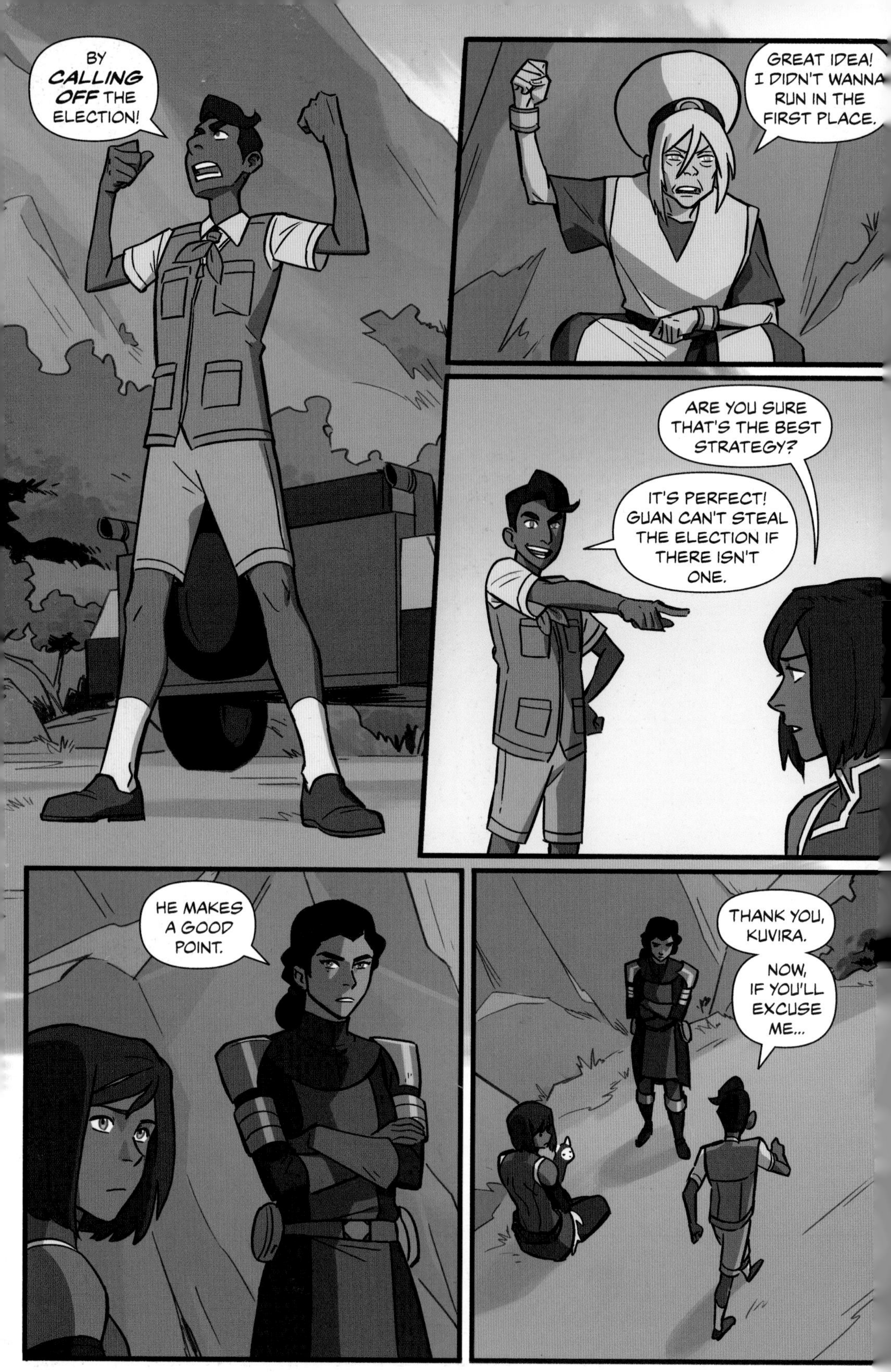
BY CALLING OFF THE ELECTION!
GREAT IDEA! I DIDN'T WANNA RUN IN THE FIRST PLACE.
ARE YOU SURE THAT'S THE BEST STRATEGY?
IT'S PERFECT! GUAN CAN'T STEAL THE ELECTION IF THERE ISN'T ONE.
HE MAKES A GOOD POINT.
THANK YOU, KUVIRA.
NOW, IF YOU'LL EXCUSE ME...

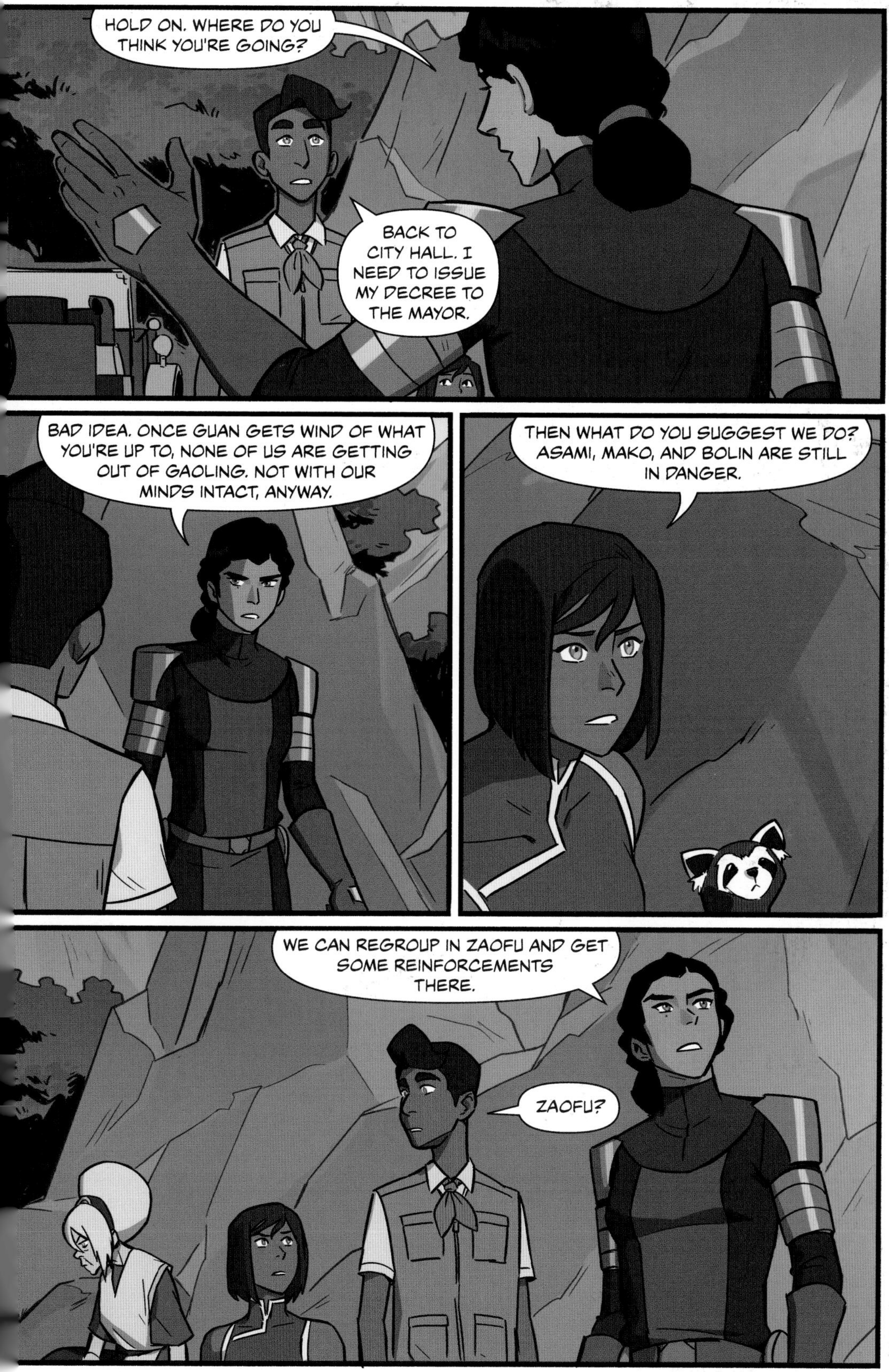
HOLD ON. WHERE DO YOU THINK YOU'RE GOING?
BACK TO CITY HALL. I NEED TO ISSUE MY DECREE TO THE MAYOR.
BAD IDEA. ONCE GUAN GETS WIND OF WHAT YOU'RE UP TO, NONE OF US ARE GETTING OUT OF GAOLING. NOT WITH OUR MINDS INTACT, ANYWAY.
THEN WHAT DO YOU SUGGEST WE DO? ASAMI, MAKO, AND BOLIN ARE STILL IN DANGER.
WE CAN REGROUP IN ZAOFU AND GET SOME REINFORCEMENTS THERE.
ZAOFU?

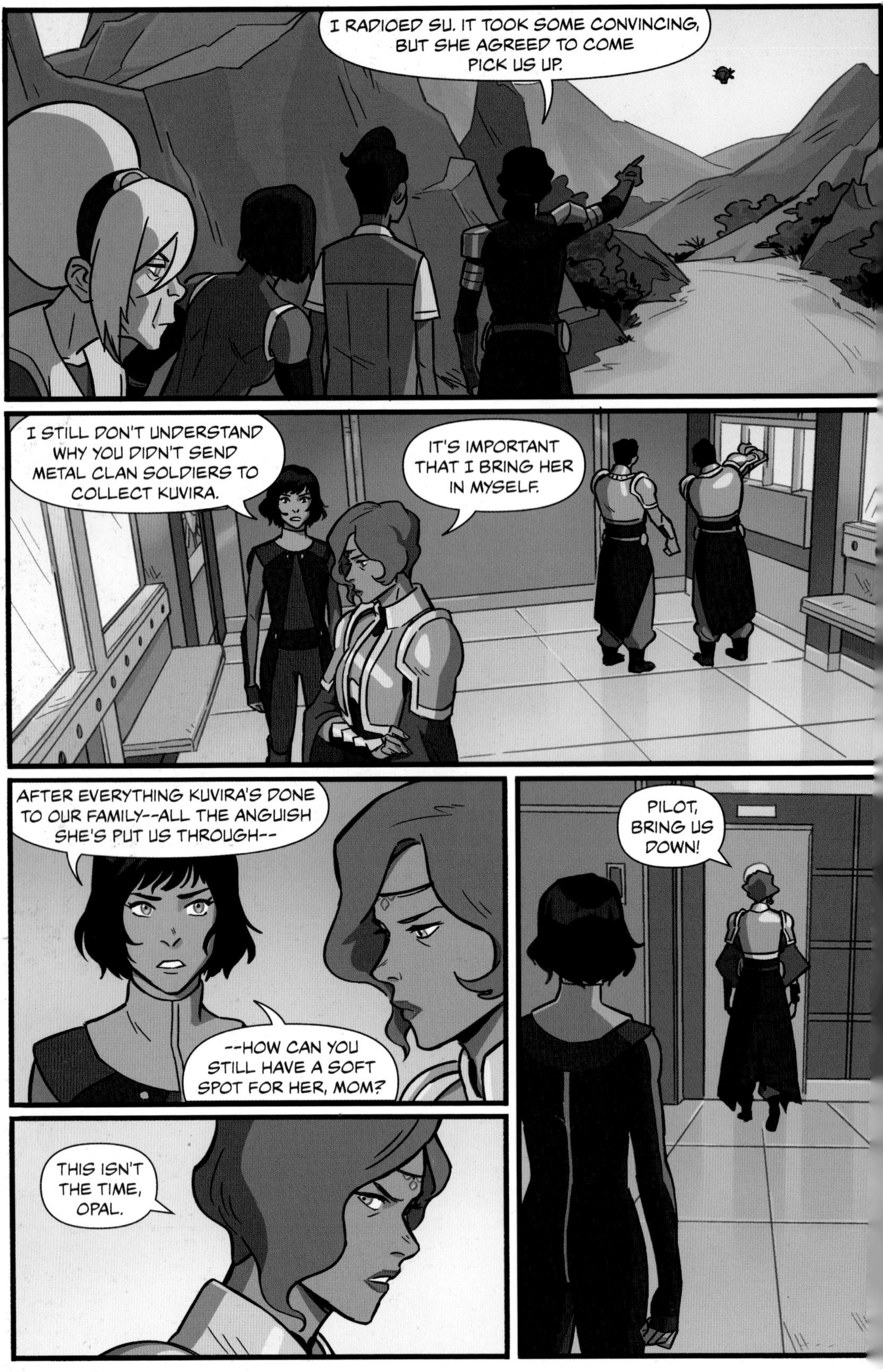
I RADIOED SU. IT TOOK SOME CONVINCING, BUT SHE AGREED TO COME PICK US UP.
I STILL DON'T UNDERSTAND WHY YOU DIDN'T SEND METAL CLAN SOLDIERS TO COLLECT KUVIRA.
IT'S IMPORTANT THAT I BRING HER IN MYSELF.
AFTER EVERYTHING KUVIRA'S DONE TO OUR FAMILY--ALL THE ANGUISH SHE'S PUT US THROUGH--
--HOW CAN YOU STILL HAVE A SOFT SPOT FOR HER, MOM?
THIS ISN'T THE TIME, OPAL.
PILOT, BRING US DOWN!

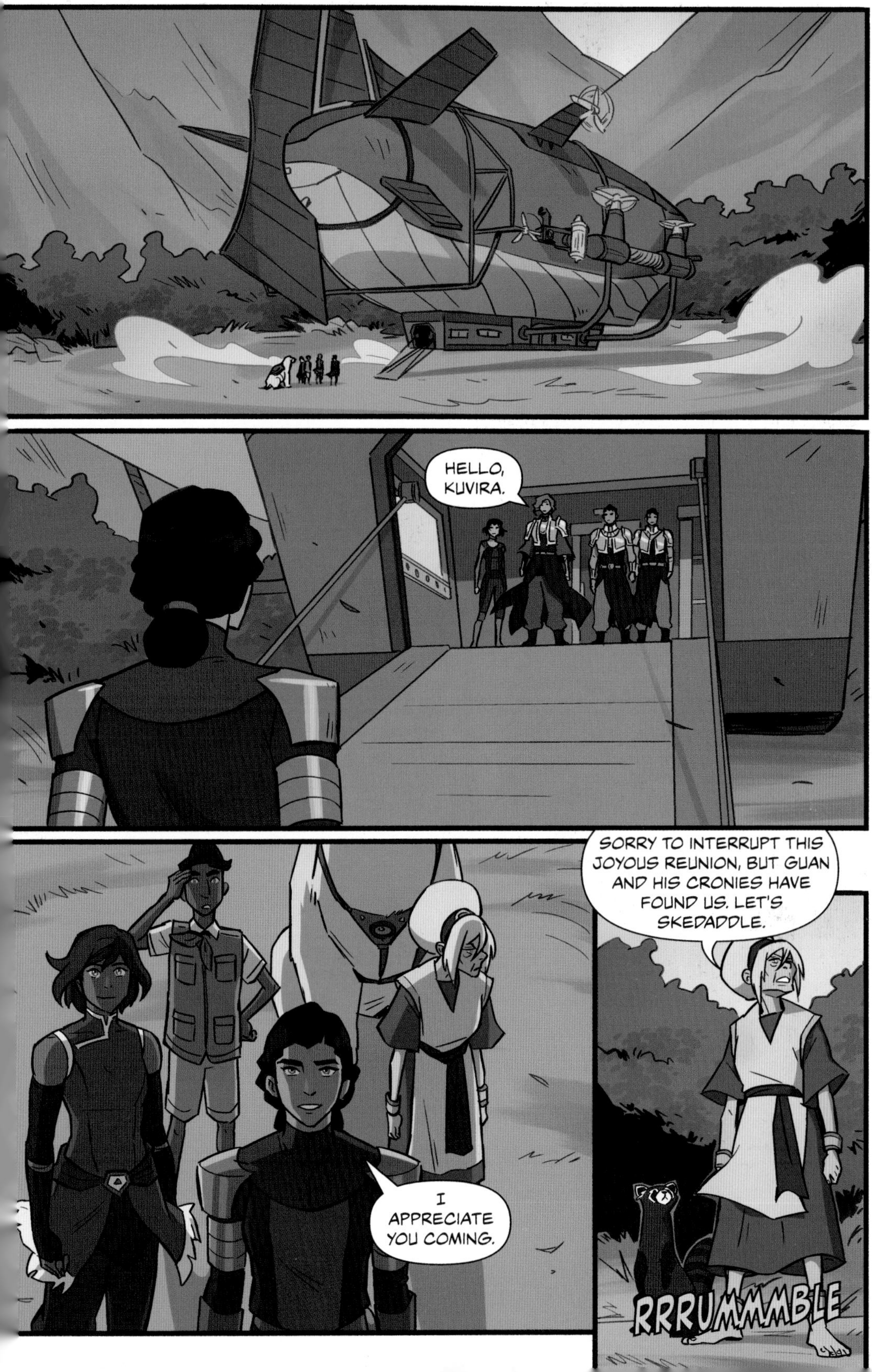
HELLO, KUVIRA.
I APPRECIATE YOU COMING.
SORRY TO INTERRUPT THIS JOYOUS REUNION, BUT GUAN AND HIS CRONIES HAVE FOUND US. LET'S SKEDADDLE.
RRRUMMMBLE

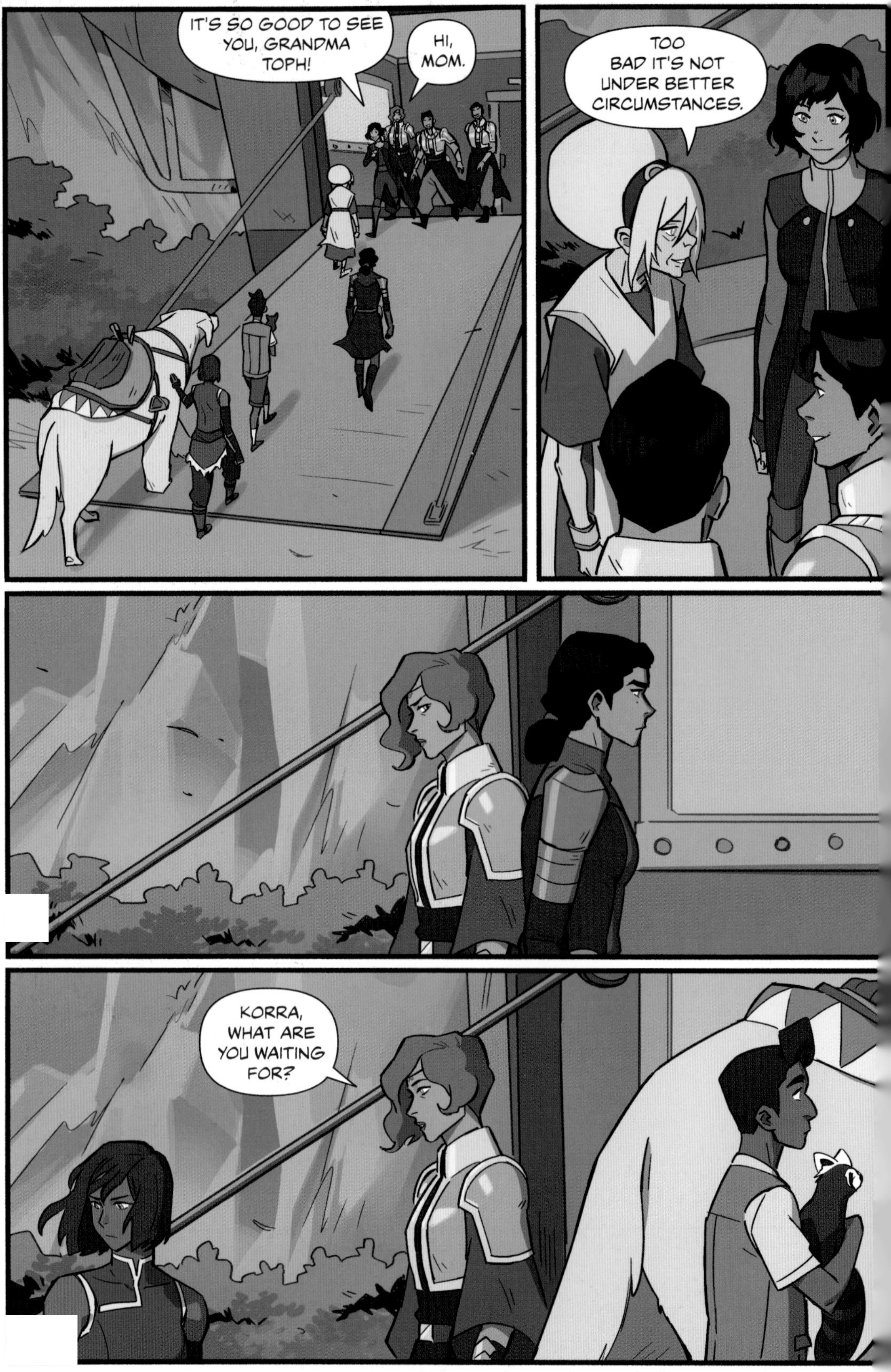
IT'S SO GOOD TO SEE YOU, GRANDMA TOPH!
HI, MOM.
TOO BAD IT'S NOT UNDER BETTER CIRCUMSTANCES.
KORRA, WHAT ARE YOU WAITING FOR?

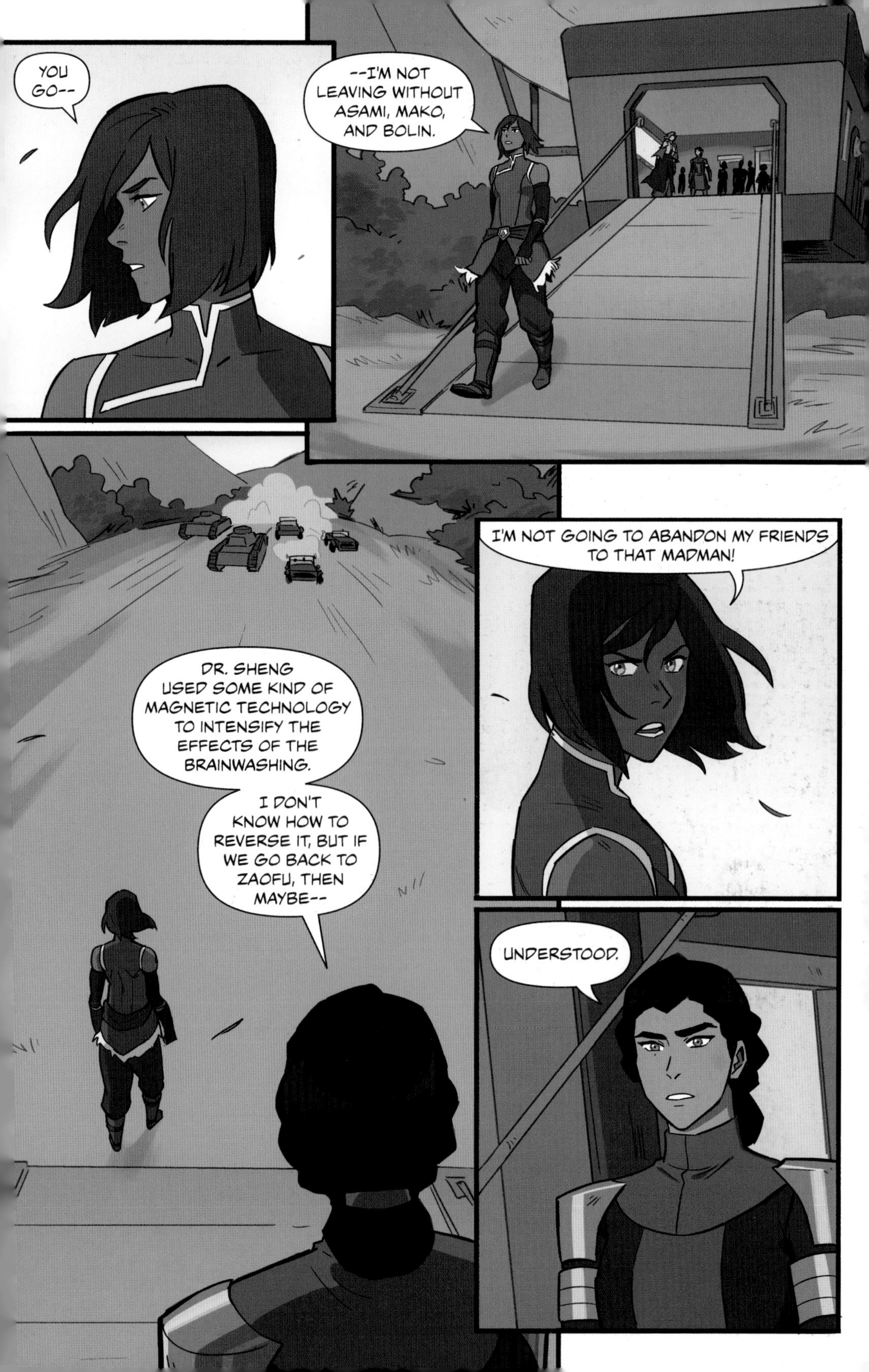
YOU GO--
--I'M NOT LEAVING WITHOUT ASAMI, MAKO, AND BOLIN.
I'M NOT GOING TO ABANDON MY FRIENDS TO THAT MADMAN!
DR. SHENG USED SOME KIND OF MAGNETIC TECHNOLOGY TO INTENSIFY THE EFFECTS OF THE BRAINWASHING.
I DON'T KNOW HOW TO REVERSE IT, BUT IF WE GO BACK TO ZAOFU, THEN MAYBE--
UNDERSTOOD.

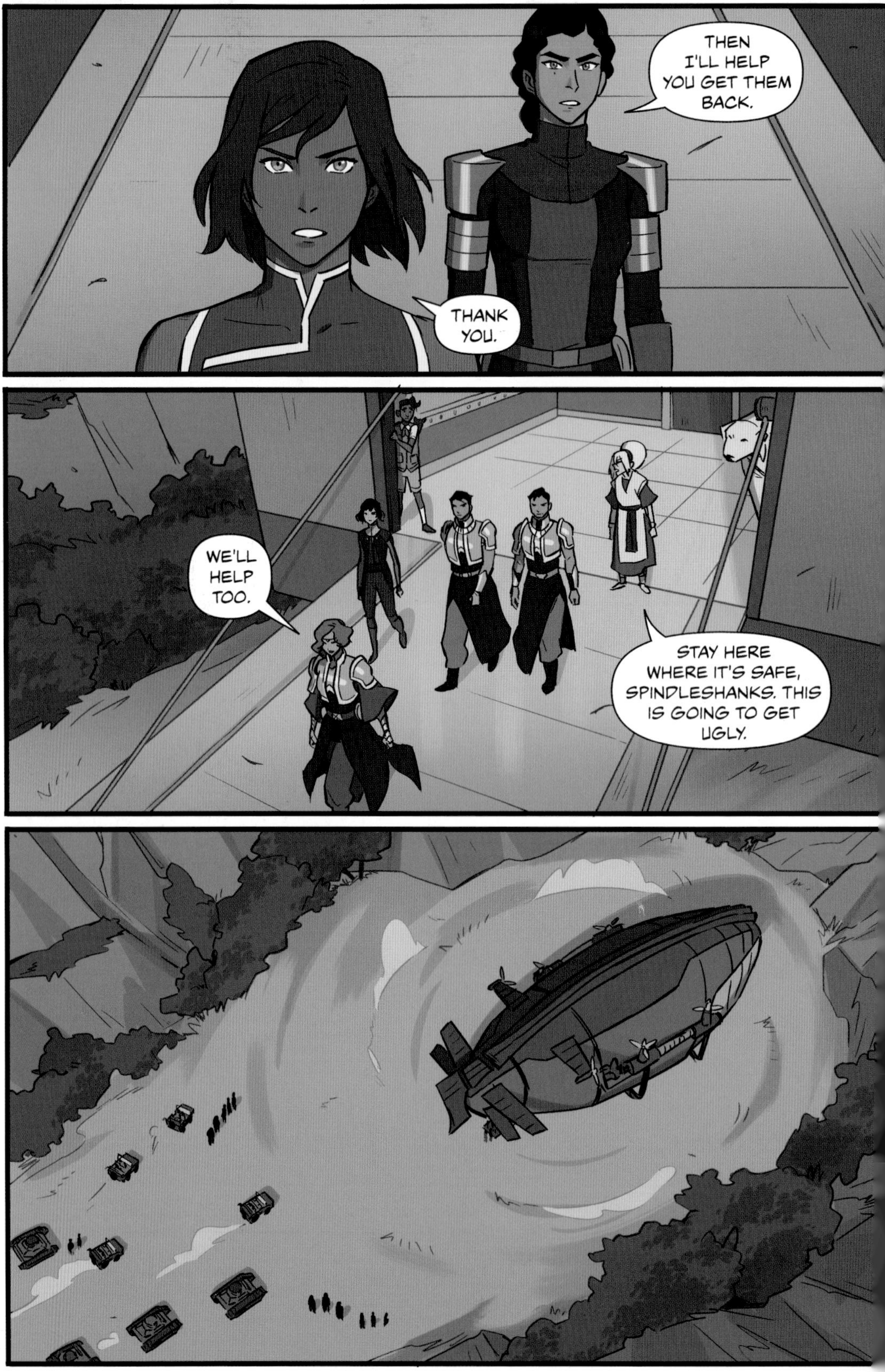
THEN I'LL HELP YOU GET THEM BACK.
THANK YOU.
WE'LL HELP TOO.
STAY HERE WHERE IT'S SAFE, SPINDLESHANKS. THIS IS GOING TO GET UGLY.

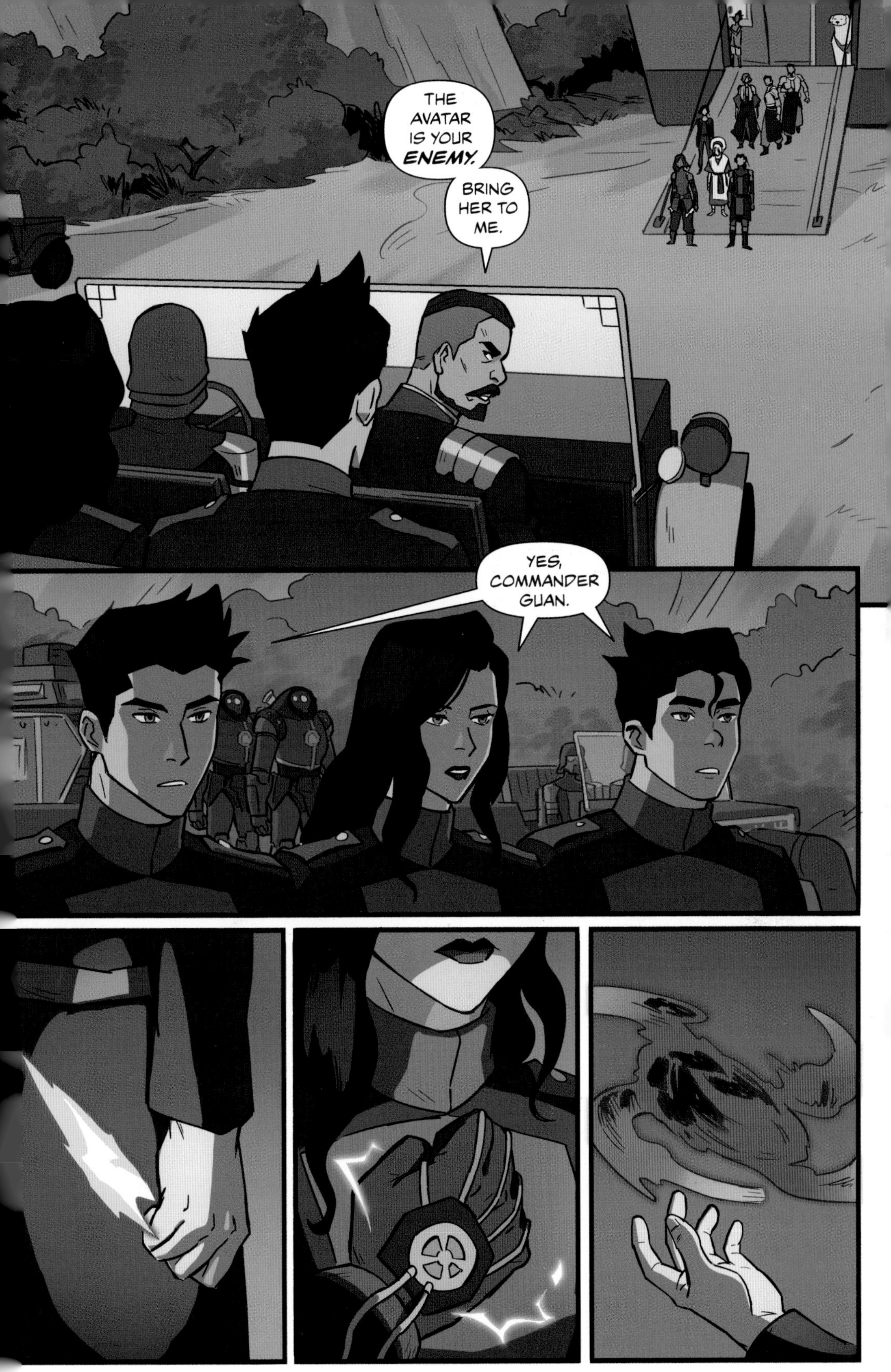
THE AVATAR IS YOUR ENEMY.
BRING HER TO ME.
YES, COMMANDER GUAN.

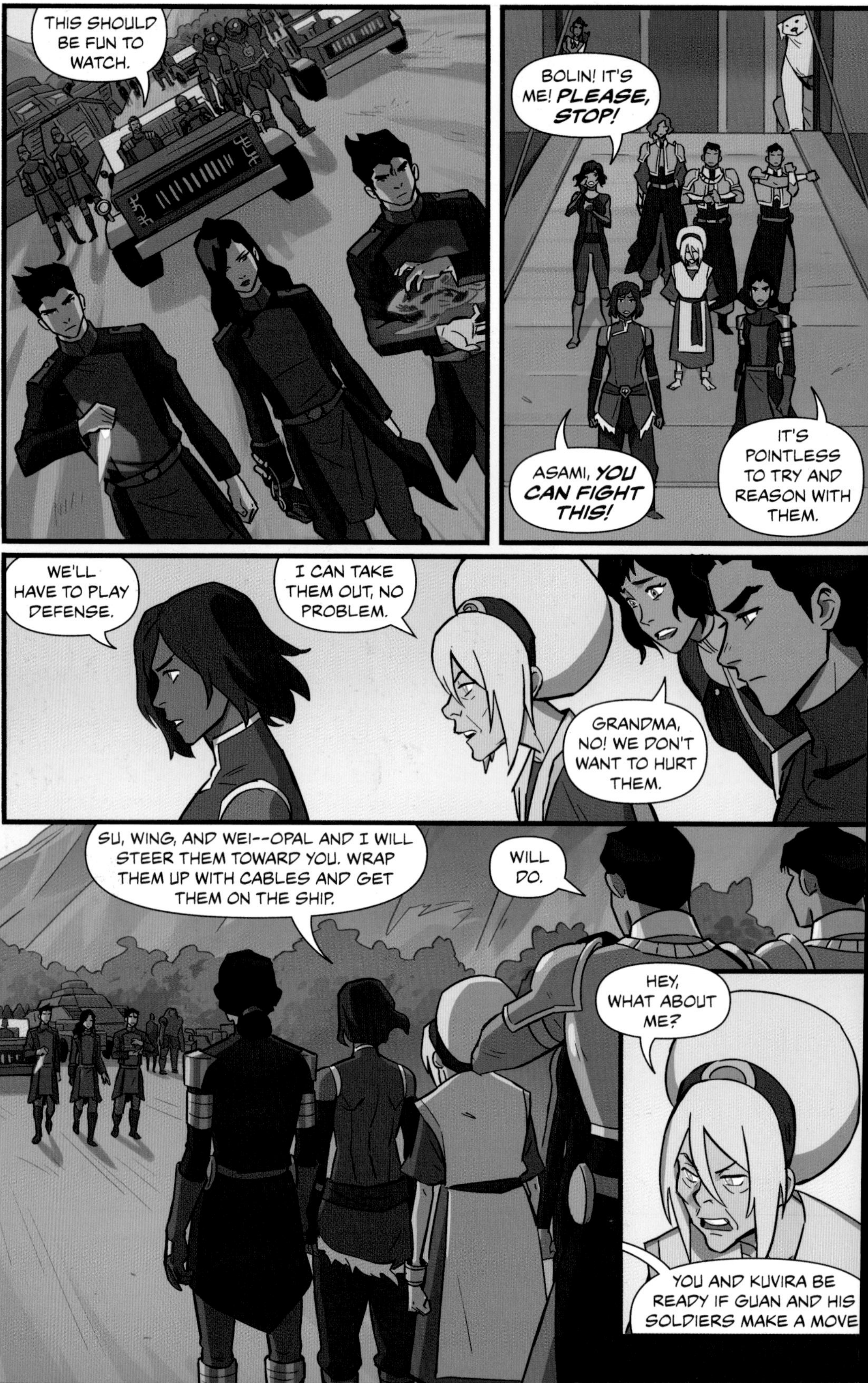
THIS SHOULD BE FUN TO WATCH.
BOLIN! IT'S ME! PLEASE, STOP!
ASAMI, YOU CAN FIGHT THIS!
IT'S POINTLESS TO TRY AND REASON WITH THEM.
WE'LL HAVE TO PLAY DEFENSE.
I CAN TAKE THEM OUT, NO PROBLEM.
GRANDMA, NO! WE DON'T WANT TO HURT THEM.
SU, WING, AND WEI--OPAL AND I WILL STEER THEM TOWARD YOU. WRAP THEM UP WITH CABLES AND GET THEM ON THE SHIP.
WILL DO.
HEY, WHAT ABOUT ME?
YOU AND KUVIRA BE READY IF GUAN AND HIS SOLDIERS MAKE A MOVE

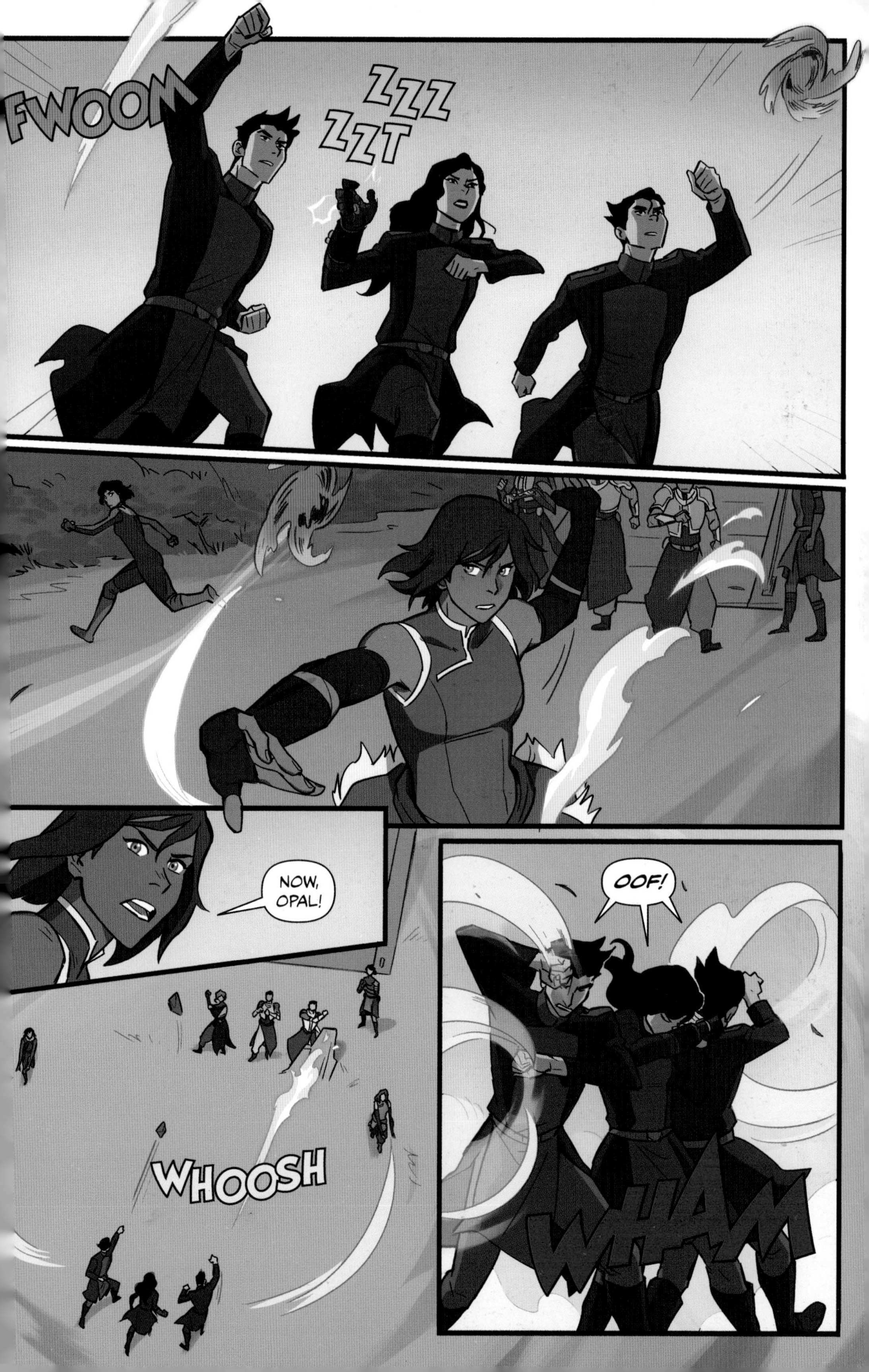
FWOOM
ZZZ
ZZT
NOW, OPAL!
WHOOSH
OOF!
WHAM

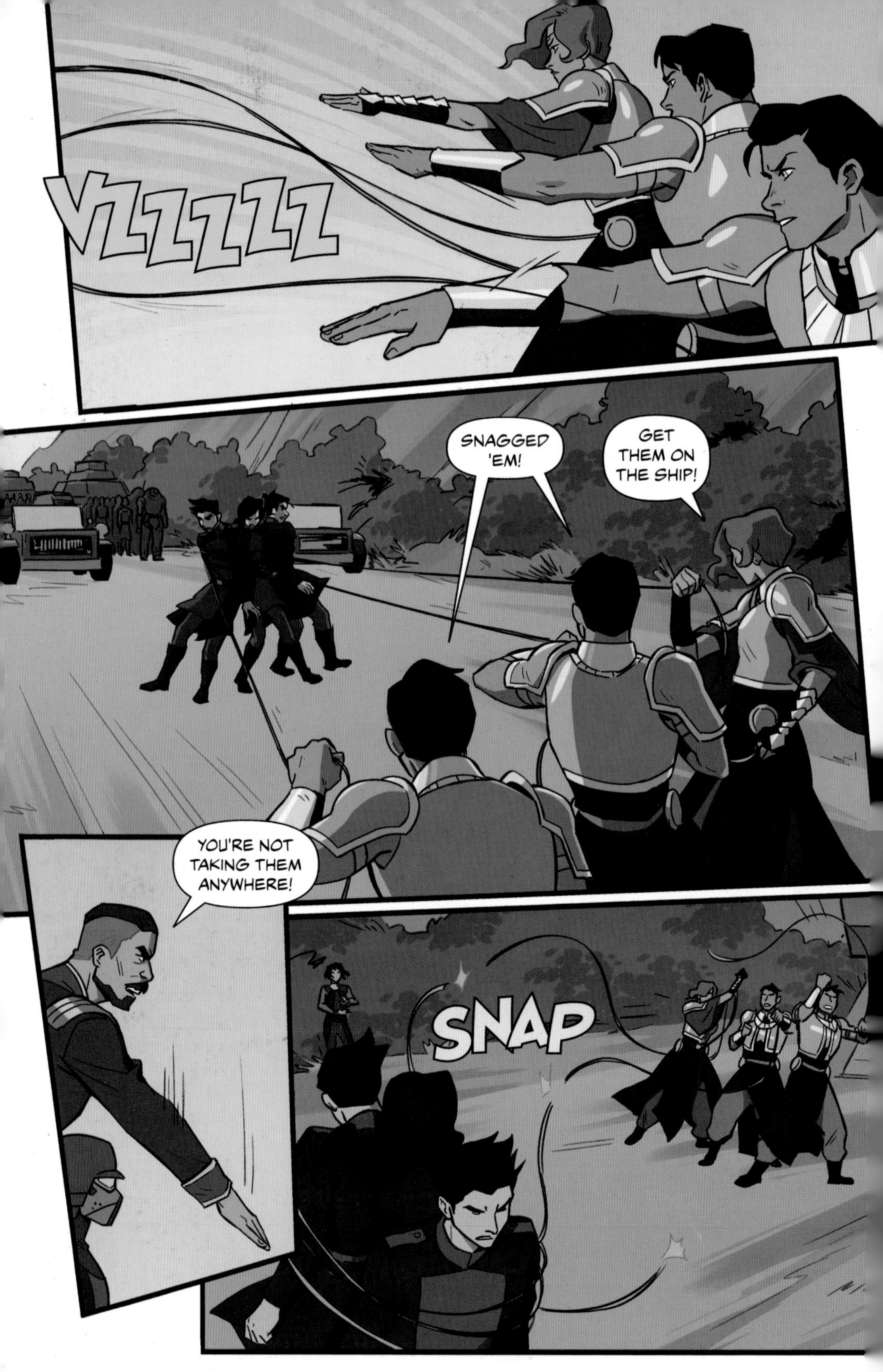
VZZZZZZ
SNAGGED 'EM!
GET THEM ON THE SHIP!
YOU'RE NOT TAKING THEM ANYWHERE!
SNAP

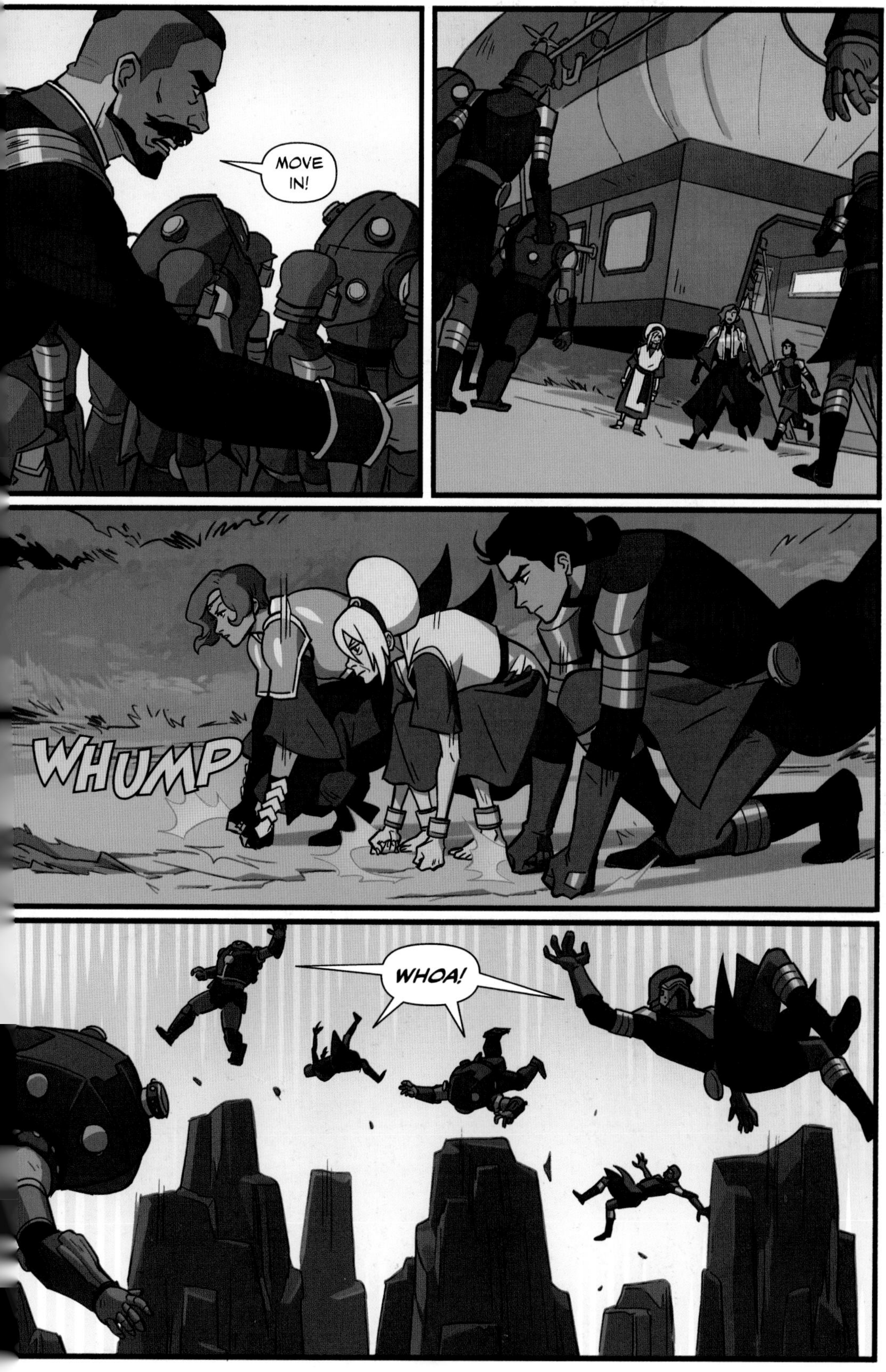
MOVE IN!
WHUMP
WHOA!

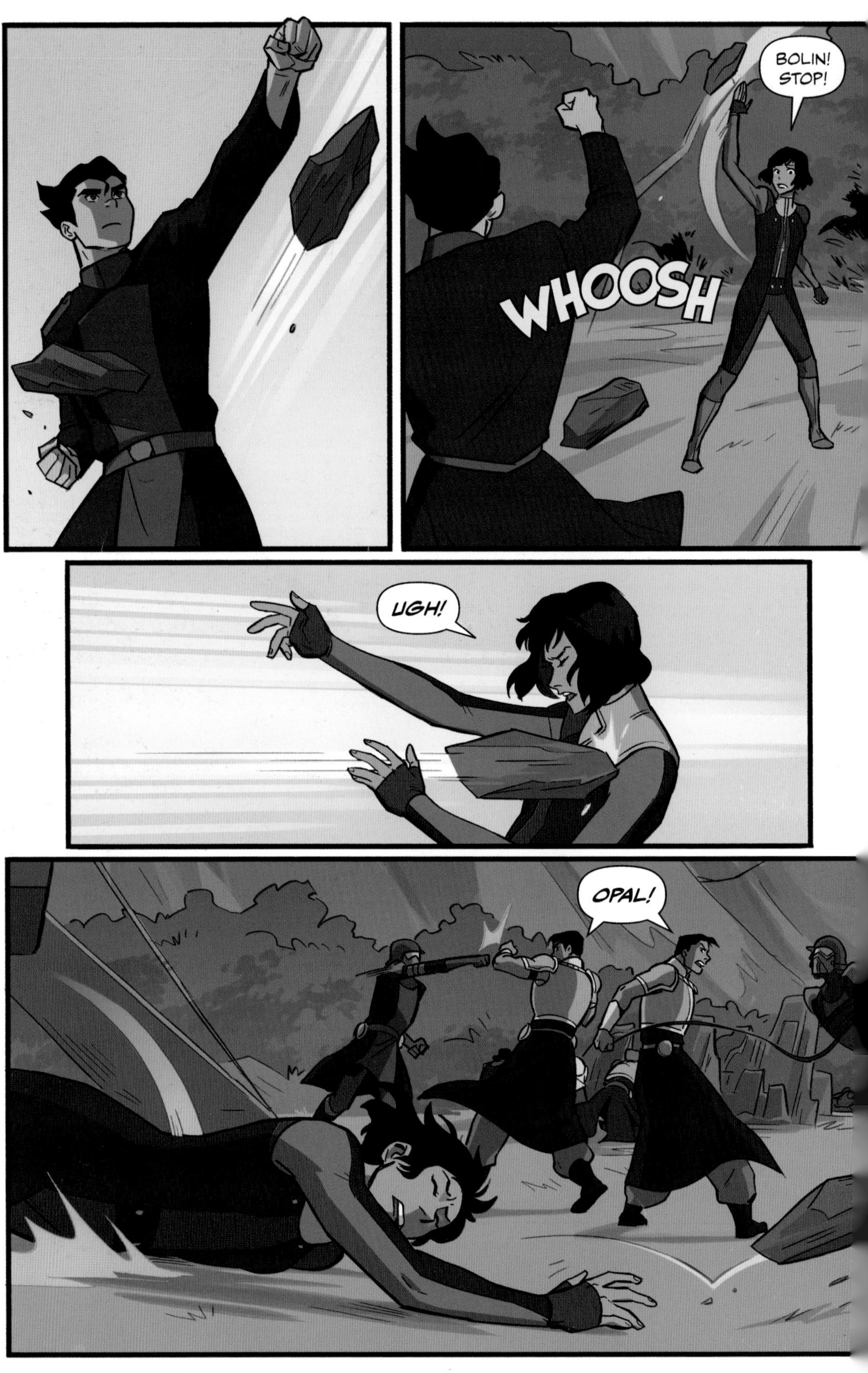
BOLIN! STOP!
WHOOSH
UGH!
OPAL!

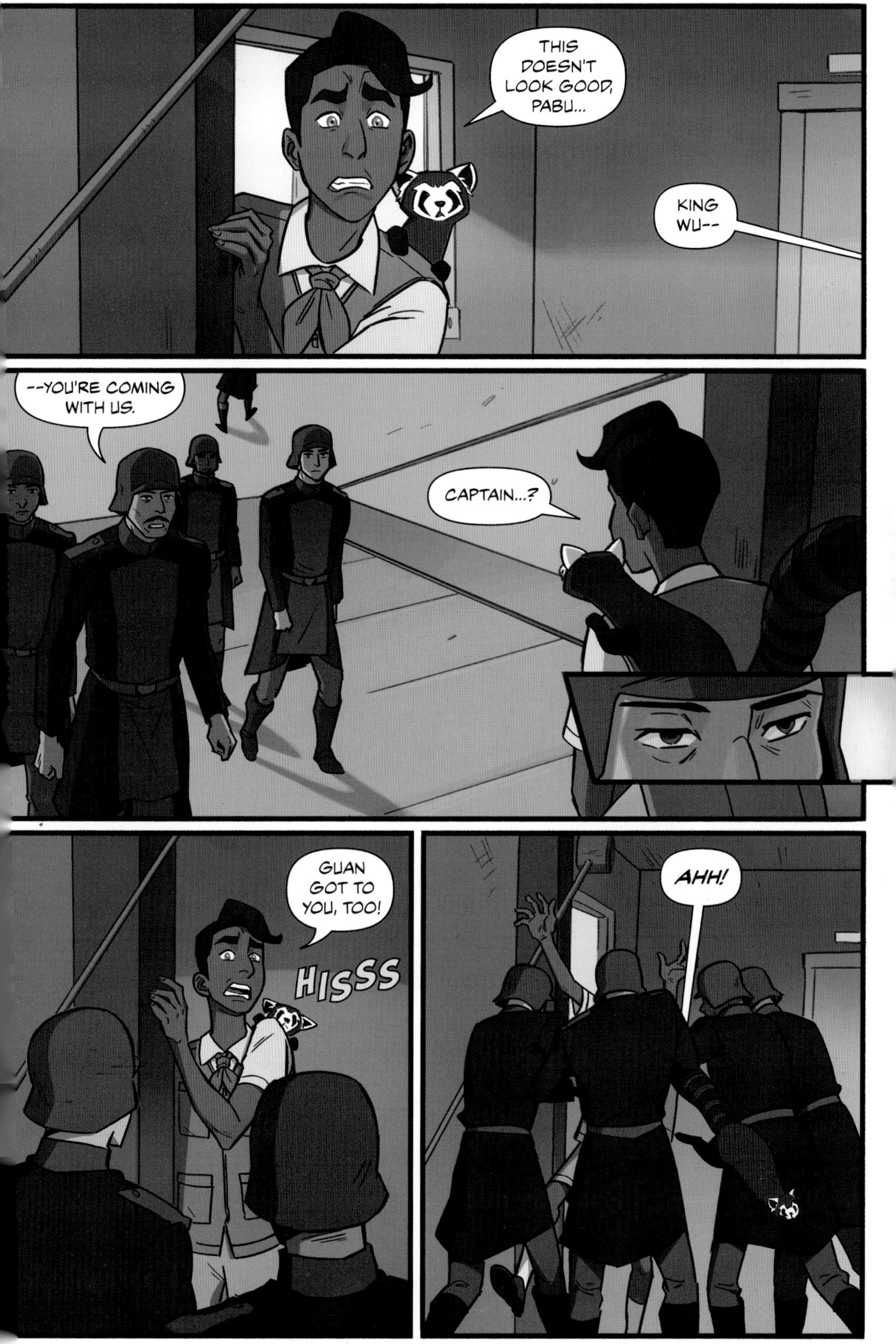
THIS DOESN'T LOOK GOOD, PABU...
KING WU--
--YOU'RE COMING WITH US.
CAPTAIN...?
GUAN GOT TO YOU, TOO!
HISSS
AHH!

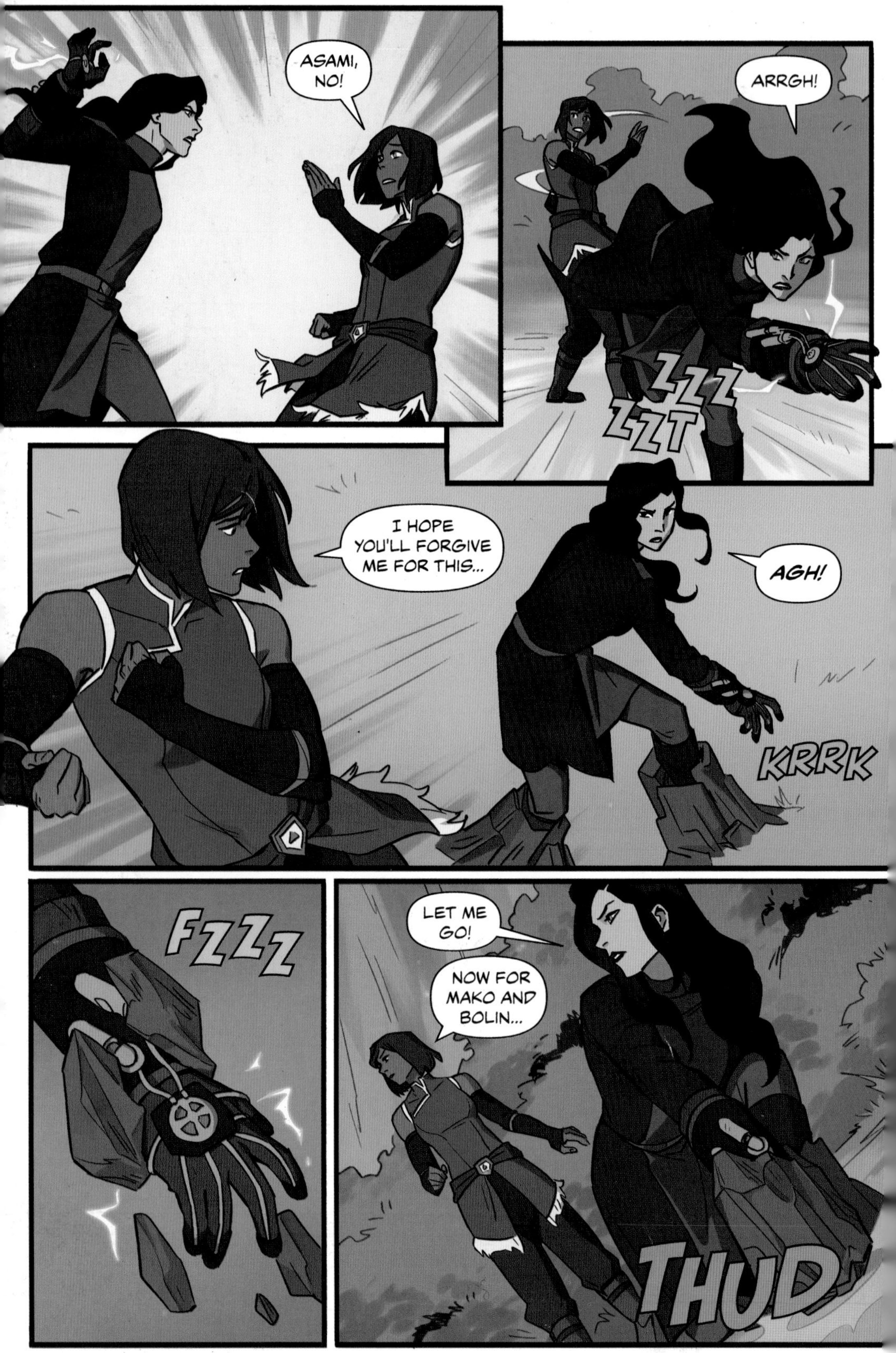
ASAMI, NO!
ARRGH!
ZZZ ZZT
I HOPE YOU'LL FORGIVE ME FOR THIS...
AGH!
KRRK
FZZZ
LET ME GO!
NOW FOR MAKO AND BOLIN...
THUD

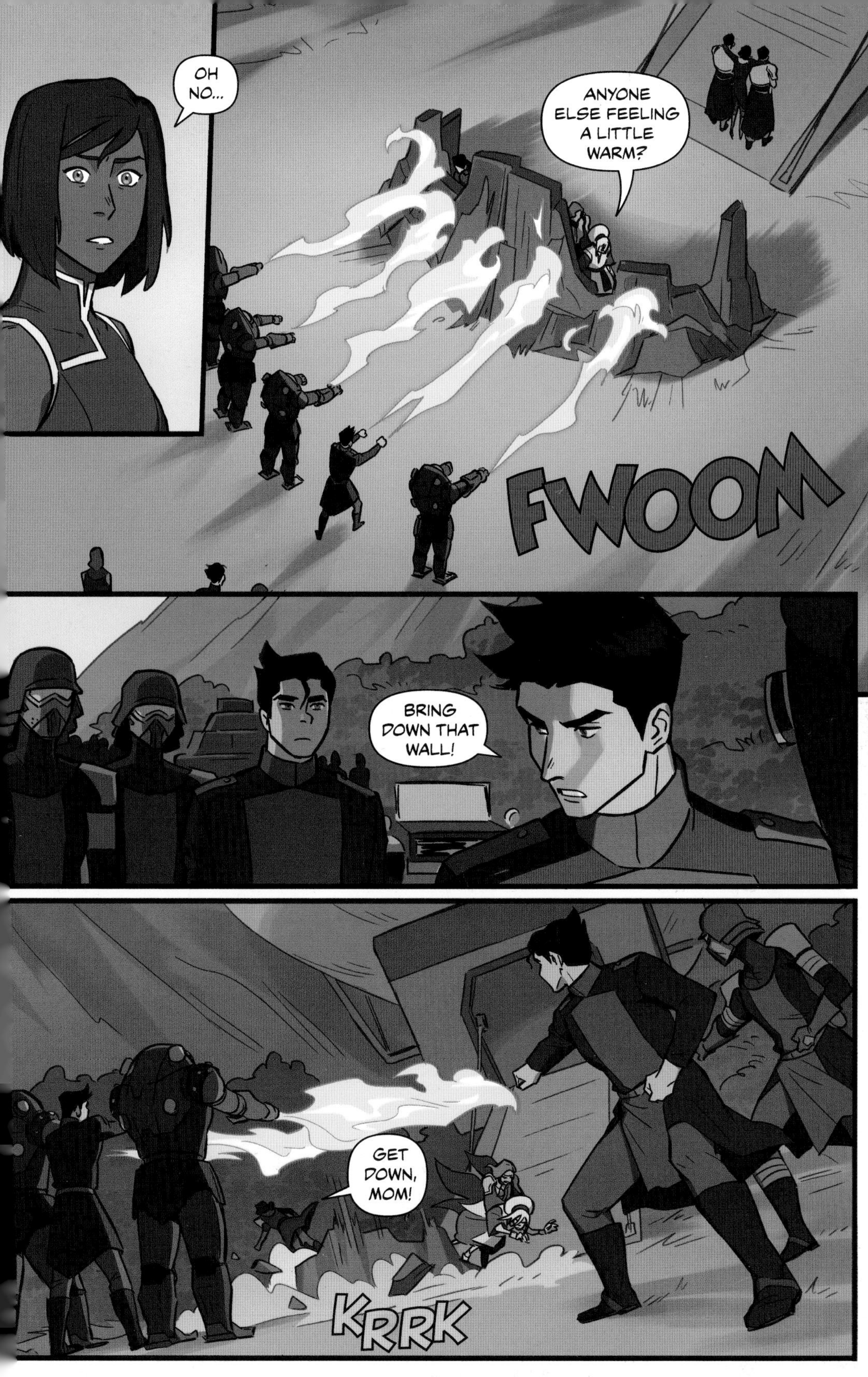
OH NO...
ANYONE ELSE FEELING A LITTLE WARM?
FWOOM
BRING DOWN THAT WALL!
GET DOWN, MOM!
KRRK

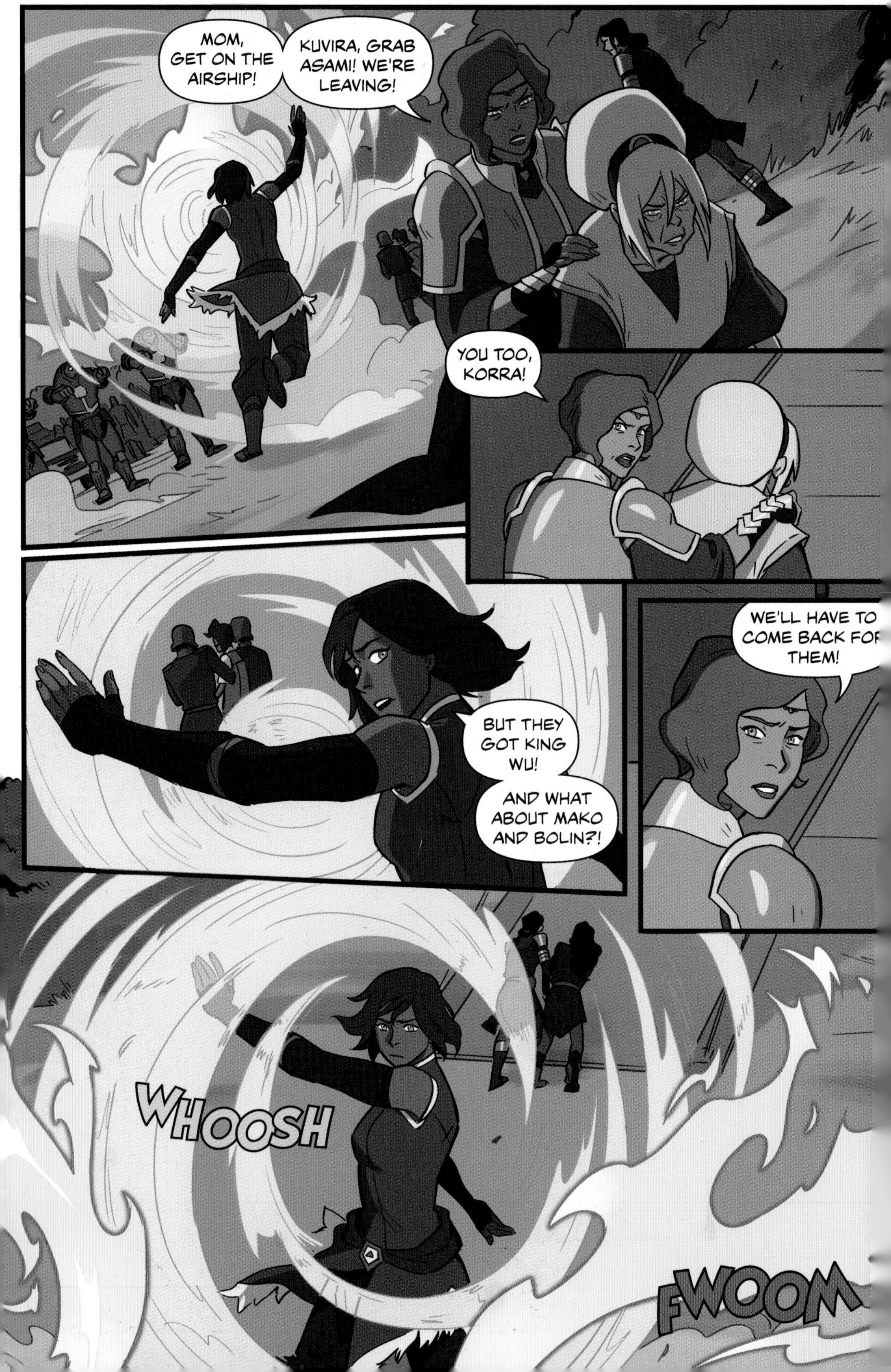
MOM, GET ON THE AIRSHIP!
KUVIRA, GRAB ASAMI! WE'RE LEAVING!
YOU TOO, KORRA!
BUT THEY GOT KING WU!
AND WHAT ABOUT MAKO AND BOLIN?!
WE'LL HAVE TO COME BACK FOR THEM!
WHOOSH
FWOOM

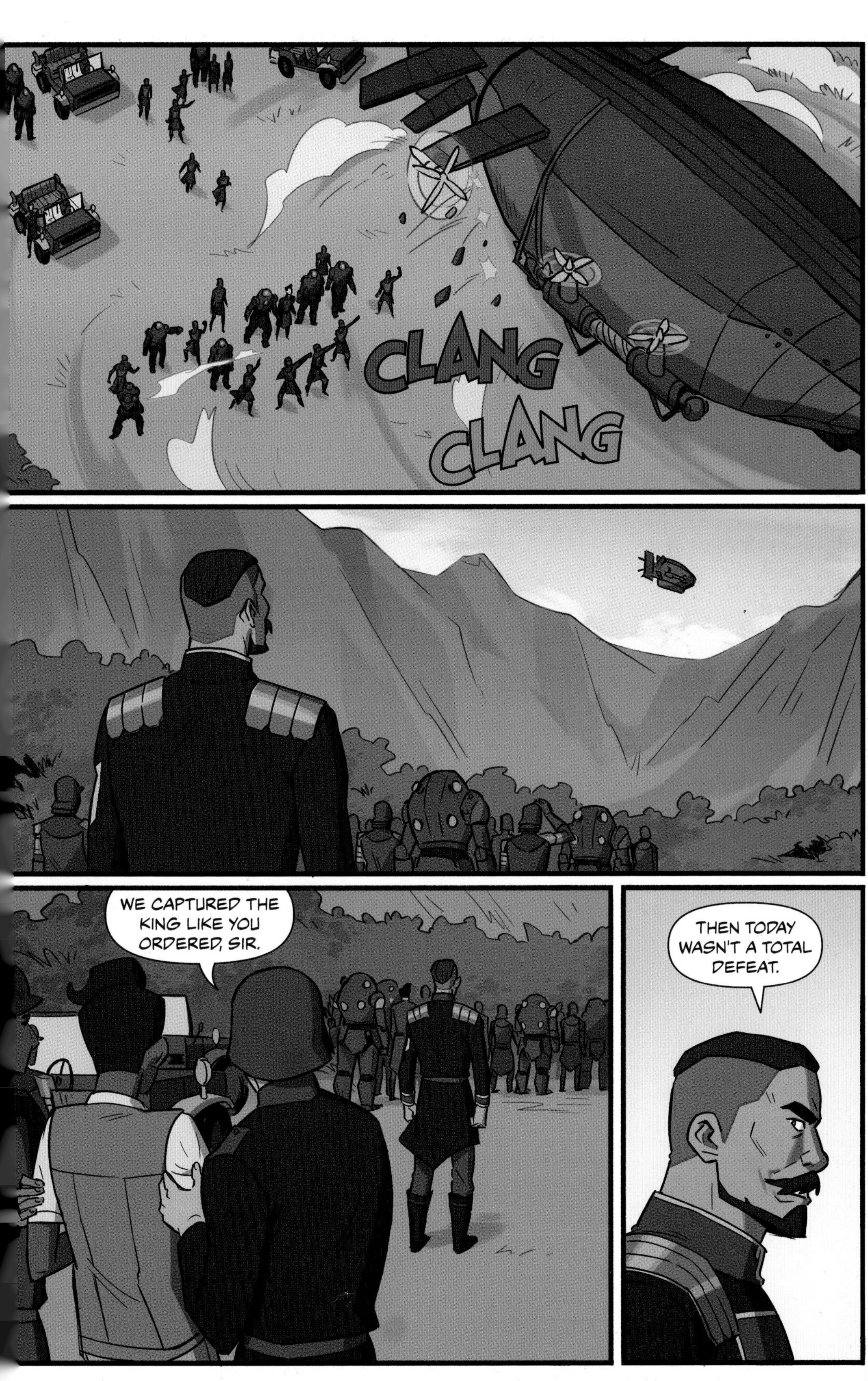
CLANG
CLANG
WE CAPTURED THE KING LIKE YOU ORDERED, SIR.
THEN TODAY WASN'T A TOTAL DEFEAT.

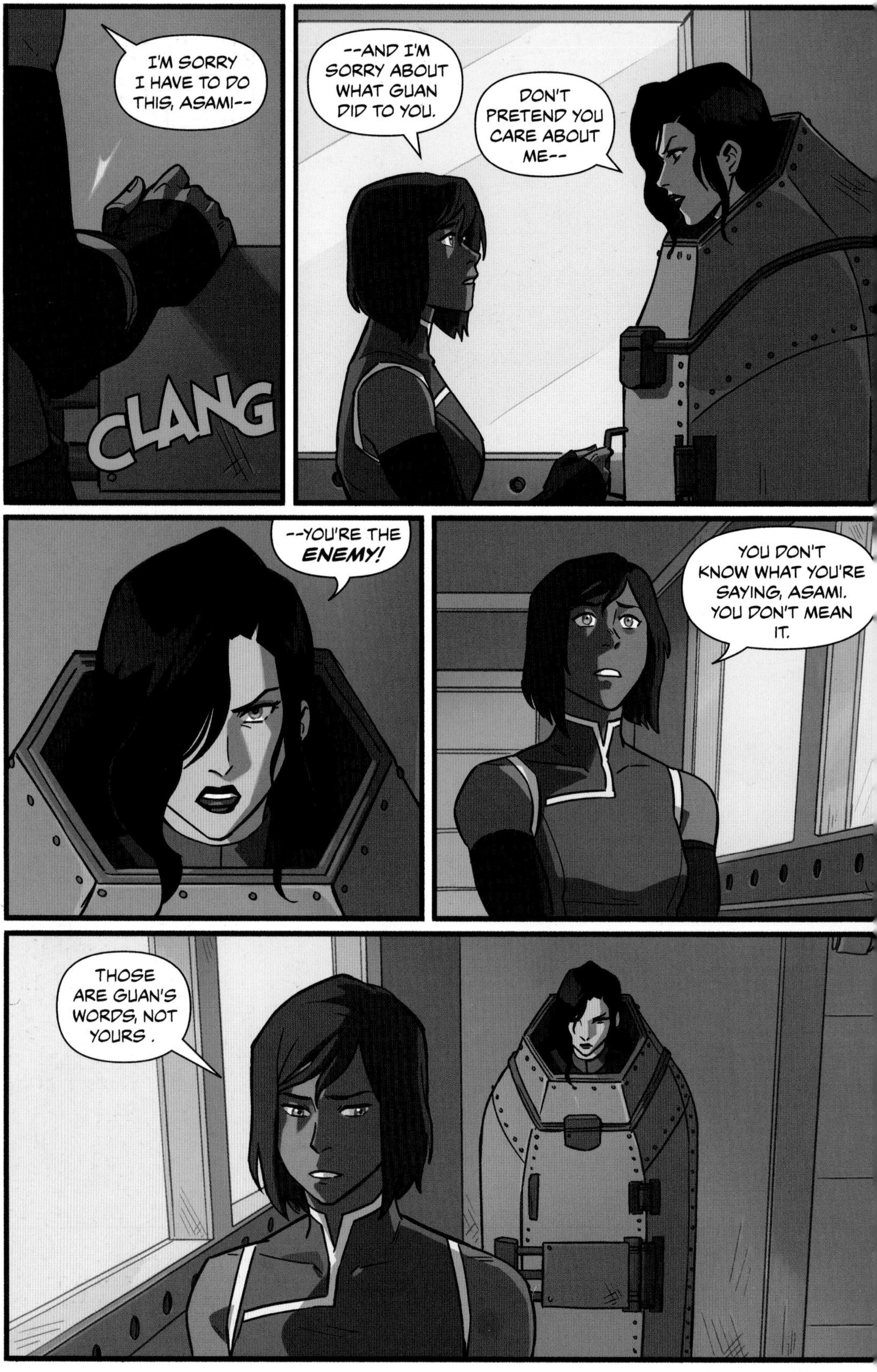
I'M SORRY I HAVE TO DO THIS, ASAMI--
CLANG
--AND I'M SORRY ABOUT WHAT GUAN DID TO YOU.
DON'T PRETEND YOU CARE ABOUT ME--
--YOU'RE THE ENEMY!
YOU DON'T KNOW WHAT YOU'RE SAYING, ASAMI. YOU DON'T MEAN IT.
THOSE ARE GUAN'S WORDS, NOT YOURS .

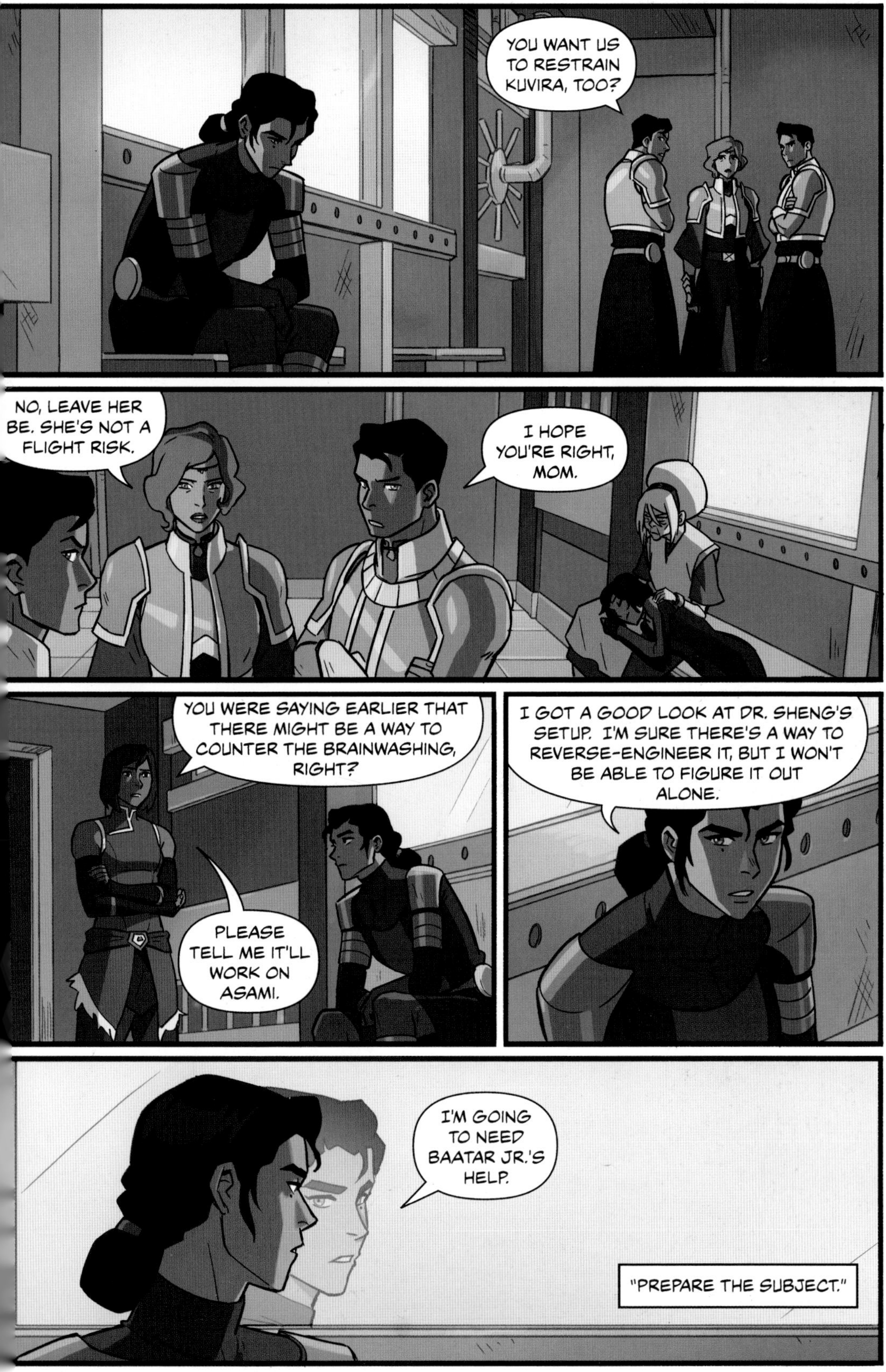
YOU WANT US TO RESTRAIN KUVIRA, TOO?
NO, LEAVE HER BE. SHE'S NOT A FLIGHT RISK.
I HOPE YOU'RE RIGHT, MOM.
YOU WERE SAYING EARLIER THAT THERE MIGHT BE A WAY TO COUNTER THE BRAINWASHING, RIGHT?
PLEASE TELL ME IT'LL WORK ON ASAMI.
I GOT A GOOD LOOK AT DR. SHENG'S SETUP. I'M SURE THERE'S A WAY TO REVERSE-ENGINEER IT, BUT I WON'T BE ABLE TO FIGURE IT OUT ALONE.
I'M GOING TO NEED BAATAR JR.'S HELP.
"PREPARE THE SUBJECT."

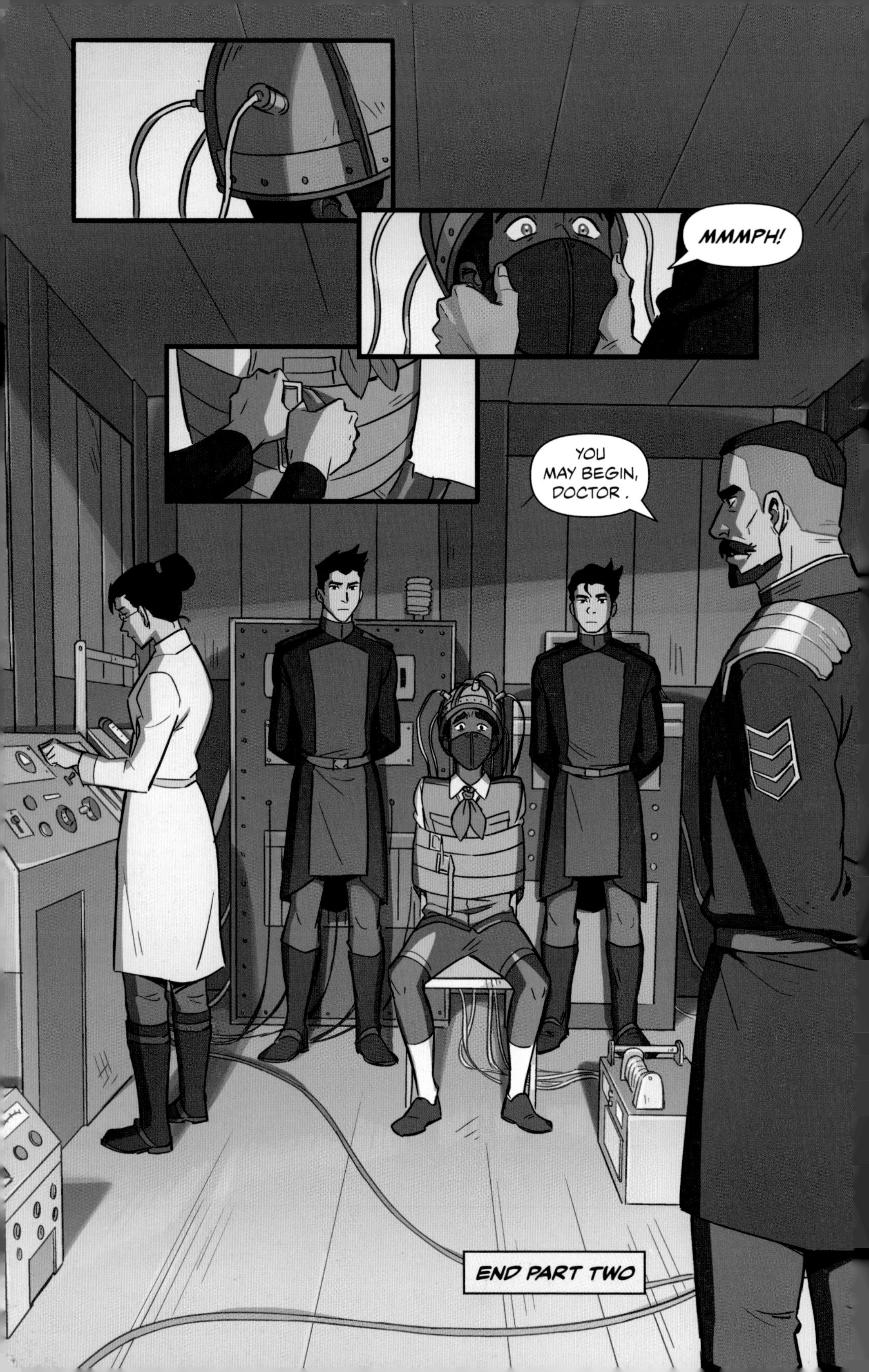
MMMPH!
YOU MAY BEGIN, DOCTOR .
END PART TWO

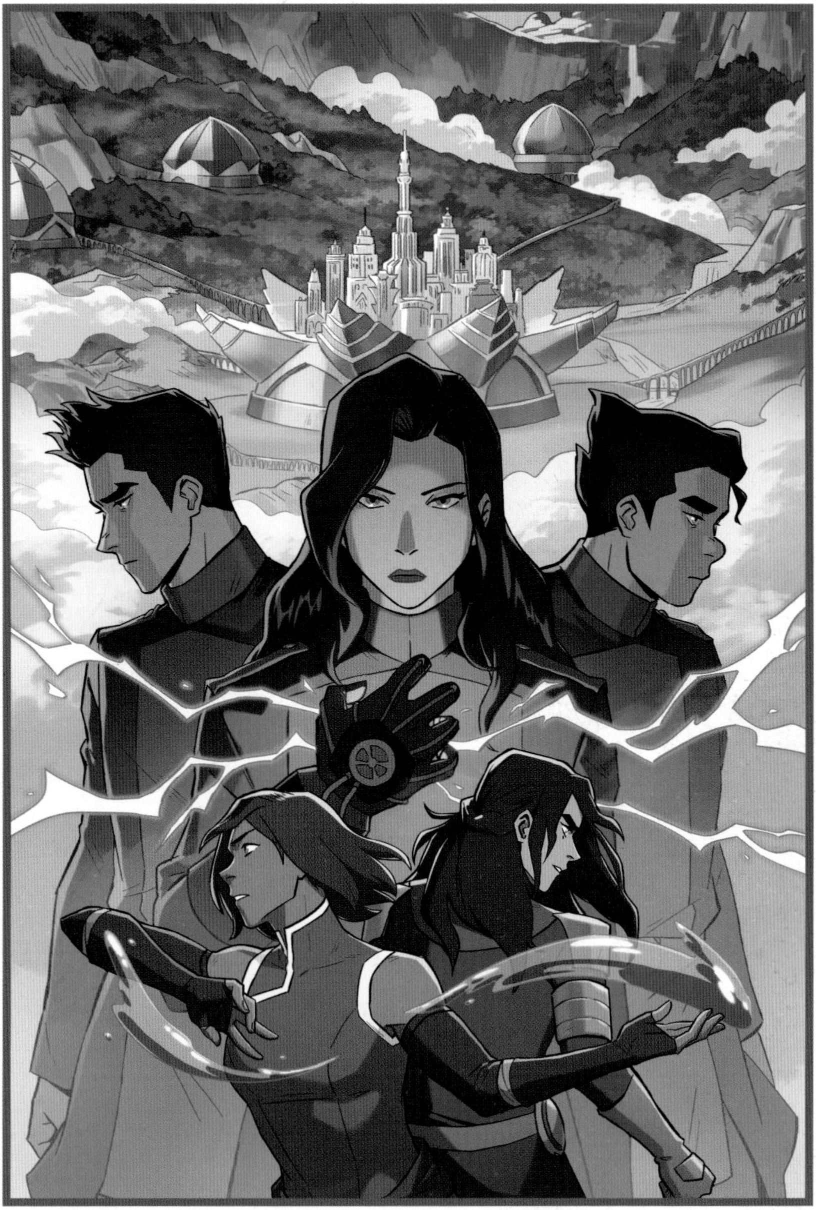

COMING IN FEBRUARY 2020!

The ultimate showdown for the Earth Kingdom's future!

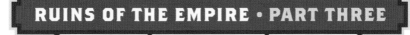

RUINS OF THE EMPIRE • PART THREE

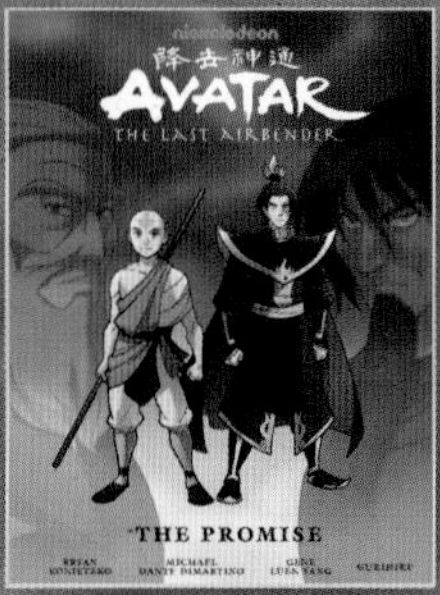
nickelodeon
AVATAR
THE LAST AIRBENDER
THE PROMISE

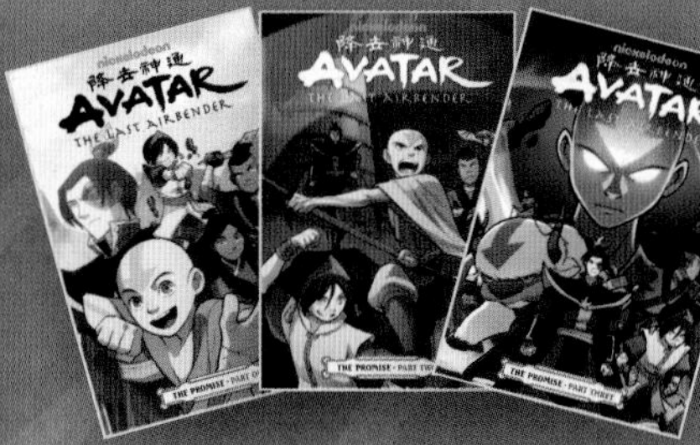
AVATAR
THE LAST AIRBENDER

Avatar: The Last Airbender—The Promise Library Edition
978-1-61655-074-5 $39.99

Avatar: The Last Airbender—The Promise Part 1
978-1-59582-811-8 $10.99

Avatar: The Last Airbender—The Promise Part 2
978-1-59582-875-0 $10.99

Avatar: The Last Airbender—The Promise Part 3
978-1-59582-941-2 $10.99

Avatar: The Last Airbender—The Search Library Edition
978-1-61655-226-8 $39.99

Avatar: The Last Airbender—The Search Part 1
978-1-61655-054-7 $10.99

Avatar: The Last Airbender—The Search Part 2
978-1-61655-190-2 $10.99

Avatar: The Last Airbender—The Search Part 3
978-1-61655-184-1 $10.99

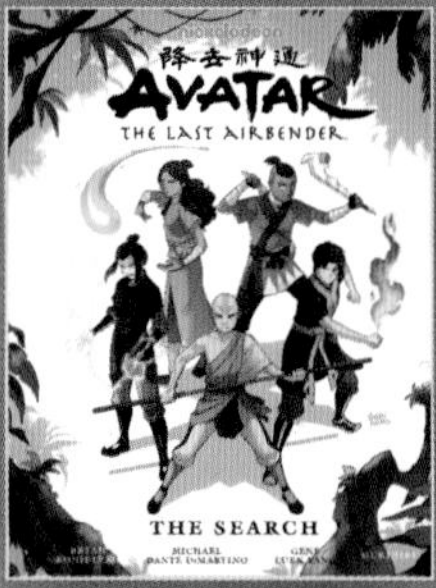
AVATAR
THE LAST AIRBENDER
THE SEARCH

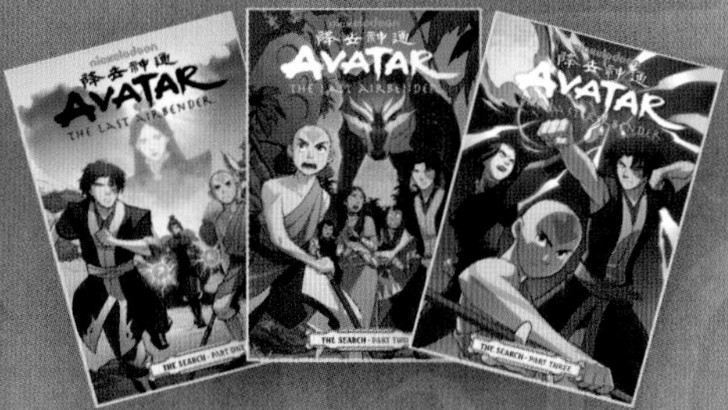
AVATAR

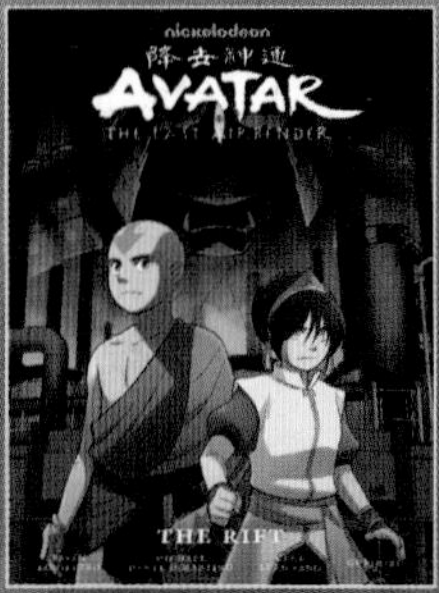
nickelodeon
AVATAR
THE RIFT

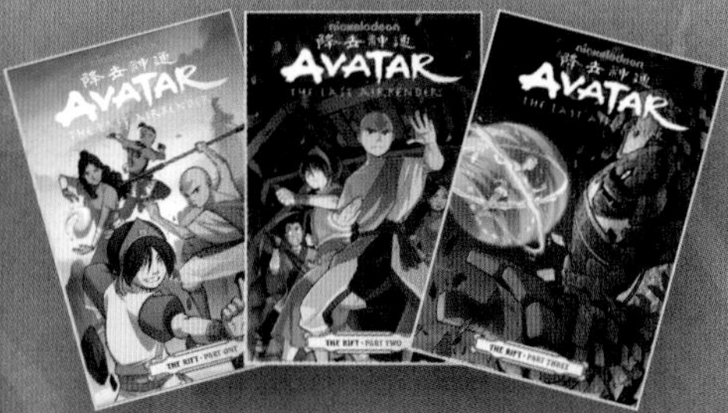
AVATAR

Avatar: The Last Airbender—The Rift Library Edition
978-1-61655-550-4 $39.99

Avatar: The Last Airbender—The Rift Part 1
978-1-61655-295-4 $10.99

Avatar: The Last Airbender—The Rift Part 2
978-1-61655-296-1 $10.99

Avatar: The Last Airbender—The Rift Part 3
978-1-61655-297-8 $10.99

Avatar: The Last Airbender—Smoke and Shadow Library Edition
978-1-50670-013-7 $39.99

Avatar: The Last Airbender—Smoke and Shadow Part 1
978-1-61655-761-4 $10.99

Avatar: The Last Airbender—Smoke and Shadow Part 2
978-1-61655-790-4 $10.99

Avatar: The Last Airbender—Smoke and Shadow Part 3
978-1-61655-838-3 $10.99

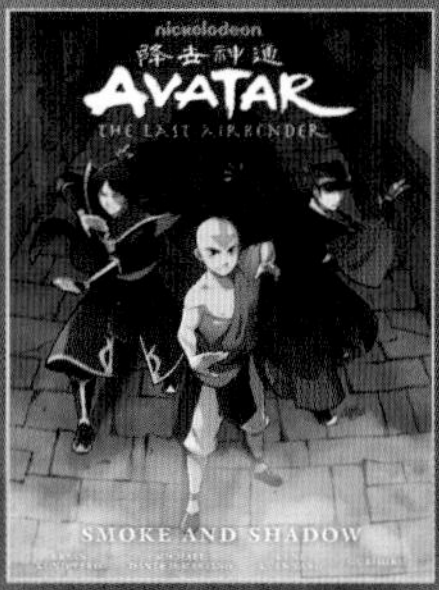
nickelodeon
AVATAR
THE LAST AIRBENDER
SMOKE AND SHADOW

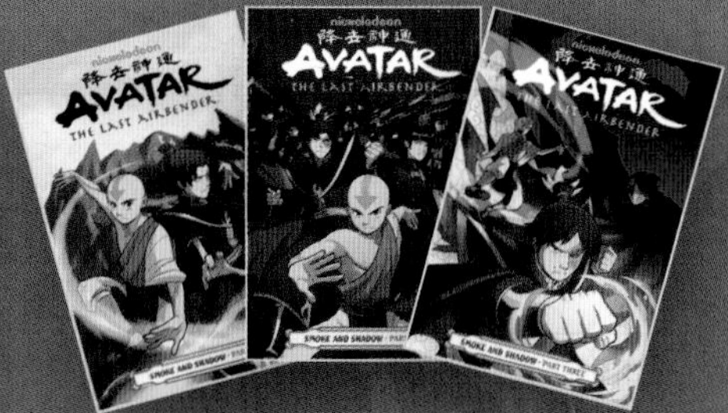
AVATAR
THE LAST AIRBENDER

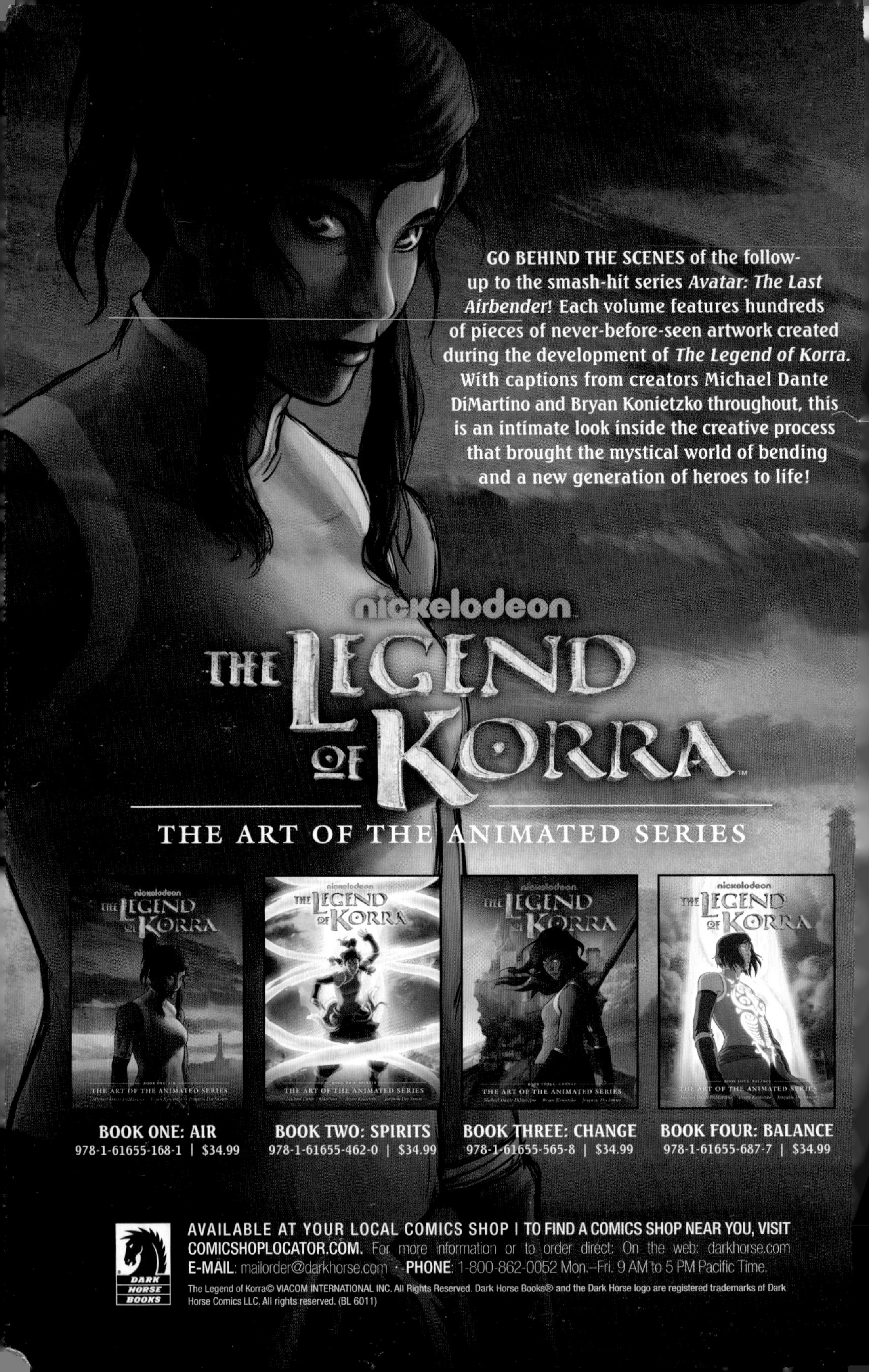
GO BEHIND THE SCENES of the follow-up to the smash-hit series Avatar: The Last Airbender! Each volume features hundreds of pieces of never-before-seen artwork created during the development of The Legend of Korra. With captions from creators Michael Dante DiMartino and Bryan Konietzko throughout, this is an intimate look inside the creative process that brought the mystical world of bending and a new generation of heroes to life!
nickelodeon
THE LEGEND OF KORRA
THE ART OF THE ANIMATED SERIES
BOOK ONE: AIR
978-1-61655-168-1 | $34.99
BOOK TWO: SPIRITS
978-1-61655-462-0 | $34.99
BOOK THREE: CHANGE
978-1-61655-565-8 | $34.99
BOOK FOUR: BALANCE
978-1-61655-687-7 | $34.99
DARK HORSE BOOKS
AVAILABLE AT YOUR LOCAL COMICS SHOP | TO FIND A COMICS SHOP NEAR YOU, VISIT COMICSHOPLOCATOR.COM. For more information or to order direct: On the web: darkhorse.com
E-MAIL: mailorder@darkhorse.com · PHONE: 1-800-862-0052 Mon.–Fri. 9 AM to 5 PM Pacific Time.
The Legend of Korra© VIACOM INTERNATIONAL INC. All Rights Reserved. Dark Horse Books® and the Dark Horse logo are registered trademarks of Dark Horse Comics LLC. All rights reserved. (BL 6011)